Endorsed by Vale T
is now recommende
students! Great introduction to the insurance claims industry, key roles, business models and an approach to build a career trajectory. An easy, fast read that will familiarize the reader with terms and processes using large and complex claims examples.

- *Doug Dell, VP at Vale Training*

GREAT BOOK! Very well written and an easy read about a complicated topic! Tim Christ nailed it!

- *Pamela Pettus, Executive Director of TheGavel.net, a national association of defense attorneys*

Came across the book one night, and found I couldn't stop reading it until I finished the whole book!..His war stories are also entertaining and page turners...The book also helped me to identify some areas I can improve upon as an engineer. Everyone can take some nuggets from this book, no matter your experience level.

- *Jeff Foster, Managing Principal at Teal Forensics*

Mr. Christ details in his book an accurate, detailed description of the forensic engineering industry and its integral connections to insurance and law. This is a worthwhile read...

Terry Taylor, P.E., Senior Principal at Haag Global

As a veteran in the forensic engineering space I found this book to be spot on regarding all aspects of the profession. If you manage a forensic engineering sales force this book is an absolute "must read" for your staff. Testifying experts will also gain knowledge as to the inner workings of both their clients (if they do insurance work) and the hurdles they will be expected to overcome. A concise and well-written read that covers all the salient issues relating to this field.

- *Jim Kelleher, LegalMetrix.com, and former Business Development Representative for both ARCCA and LWG Consulting*

Very thorough analysis and good real-life examples!

- *Bob Wilens, Subrogation attorney at Thompson Brody & Kaplan*

Tim is very in tune with what differentiates "expert" from "world-class expert." This is a great application of years of experience providing experts!

- *Janel Giarratano, CEO of Forte Consulting & Investigations*

A complete review of wide-ranging forensic investigations compiled over many years...I heartily recommend this book.

- *John Griffith, Ph.D., P.E., Senior Engineer & Associate Professor, Nicholls State University*

Becoming a World-Class Expert:
The Business of Forensic Engineering

by
Timothy D. Christ, M.B.A.

Copyright © 2018 by Timothy D. Christ, M.B.A.
All rights reserved. No part of this book may be reproduced, scanned, or distributed in any printed or electronic form without permission.
First Edition: January 2018
Printed in the United States of America

Becoming an Expert: The Business of Forensic Engineering

Table of Contents

Table of Contents v
Dedication vi
Preface ix
   Why Forensic Engineering? 10
   Understanding the Insurance Business Model 18
   Understanding the Insurance Claims Process 32
   The Various Types of Claims 44
   The Scientific Method 53
   Differences in Various Service Providers 58
   Great Fire Investigation 65
   Structural Engineering Cases 70
   Construction Cases 73
   Mechanical Engineering Cases 80
   Electrical Engineering Cases 84
   Petroleum Engineering Cases 88
   Environmental Engineering Cases 94
   Vehicle Accident Reconstruction Cases 98
   Cyber and Fidelity Cases 102
   Project Management on Large Losses 107
   The London Market 111
   The Basics of Litigation 117
   Building a Great Engineering Team 126
   The Changing Landscape of Insurance 130
   Conclusion 134
   About the Author 149

Timothy D. Christ, M.B.A.

Dedication

I dedicate this book to God and three people.

Dear Father, thank you very much for the opportunity to learn, interact, develop, and serve all of Your people that I came into contact with in the forensic engineering business. Thank you for keeping me safe, whether in the wilds of Honduras or the streets of London. Thank you for giving me the unique skill set to understand, to teach, to inspire, and to build a world-class forensic engineering team.

My good friend and colleague, Nagib "Tony" Elarba, P.E. (Nov 3, 1956-May 9, 2017) You were gone too soon, amigo. Thank you for taking me under your wing back in 2001 and helping to teach me all about the world of Mechanical Engineering and Forensic Engineering. You cut your teeth on the $300 million Dole claim in Guatemala and Honduras after Hurricane Mitch, and then you continued to learn on your many journeys into Venezuela, Argentina, Bolivia, Chile, Nicaragua, Mexico, and others. You were the best friend a guy could ask for. You never got tired of answering my questions or explaining things to me that

Becoming an Expert: The Business of Forensic Engineering

I didn't understand. You were a key individual of my reason to go build a Latin America business. I wanted to build an opportunity for you where you could be completely happy with your professional skills. I'm so happy that we were able to make that a reality in 2012. You got to do what you were meant to do, and there is no greater joy on this earth than to have complete alignment of your passion, skill set, and expertise. This book is dedicated to you, so that it can teach those who come after me, in the same manner with which you taught me. Thank you for your friendship and all the good times that we spent together. Every single one of our trips down south was a pleasure because we went together, and your laugh, your sense of humor, and your appetite for new experiences was exactly like mine. We could read each other's minds and on many occasions, did finish each other's sentences.

My good friend and colleague, Ricardo Torres, CFI. When I hired you in 2006, I knew that you could be a rock-star and become the premier fire investigator in Latin America. Within two years, we were well on our way, having worked over 20 large fire losses (in excess of $50 million in claim) and now, 12 years later, you are the CEO of the company we built from scratch. I am so immensely proud of you and want to thank you for all you did. You taught me how an excellent fire

Timothy D. Christ, M.B.A.

investigator does his job, you taught me about the Latin culture, and we learned together how we could succeed in Latin America. We climbed the mountain together, and I wouldn't have wanted anyone else by my side. You are the best friend a person could ask for, and we never had a dull moment. This book is dedicated to you, thank you for your wisdom, your patience, and your passion. I'm so happy to see all that you have been able to accomplish.

    My wife, Betty. I always joke that I had to move to San Antonio to find my hometown love story, but it's the truth. Thank you for being supportive of me while I pursued by professional passion. Thank you for being patient on all those long trips down south, to Canada, London, Norway, and all over the US. I think you enjoyed the New York trips more since you got to see all the Christmas lights and shop in the multi-story Macy's. I know you enjoyed the Chicago trips because of Garrett's popcorn. Thank you for blessing us with our son Kaleb, who we are working hard to grow into a responsible, independent, and driven young man.

Preface

There is no "universal standard" by which forensic engineering firms are judged. There are a ton of opinions, relationships, and other skewed perspectives. In this book, you go behind-the-scenes, deep into the world of insurance claims, litigation, and forensic engineering, and see things in the light of day. This is a pull-no-punches, hard critique of some of the best of the best, and worst of the worst. Hopefully, this book provides an excellent "big picture" perspective on the whole industry and business challenges, allowing the reader to both understand the dynamics at play as well as develop their own appropriate strategy to win.

Timothy D. Christ, M.B.A.

Chapter 1:

WHY FORENSIC ENGINEERING?

This is my Martin Luther King, "I have a dream" speech. I firmly believe, and Jim Collins backs me up in his book *Good to Great* when he talks about the Hedgehog Concept, that a person has to truly love what they are doing in order to develop to world-class. Without passion, whenever you hit a significant roadblock, you will not care enough to keep at it until you figure out a way over, around, or through it.

I was hired by Alan Barnes back in 2001 right at the height of the "mold crisis" in South Texas. We met on the Cimarron golf course down near McAllen, Texas. He found out about my Business Administration and Marketing degree and said, "I want you to come in, learn what forensic engineers do, and then I want you to go sell it." I told him, no thanks, I'm a professional golfer. I don't need to go into business. Famous last words... He kept after me for about six months and I finally gave in.

My first day was a Monday and I went out with a Structural Engineer and an Industrial Hygienist to learn how to conduct mold investigations. Technically there were two investigations going on per property: 1) The structural engineering investigation of the causes of water damage to the home, the extent of damage, the repair/replacement options, including cost estimates, and 2) The environmental engineering investigation into the possible presence of excessive mold levels in the home, and if so, the causes, extent of damage, the cleaning/decontamination options, and the costs of each.

Three days later, I was training another Structural Engineer and an Industrial Hygienist to do what I had just learned how to do three days earlier. It makes no sense looking back on it, but in the moment, we were absolutely swamped with work, and that was how we responded to it.

I fell in love with the "investigation" part of it. I've always loved the *Hardy Boys'* series, all Sherlock Holmes movies, all *CSI* and *Law & Order* shows, as well as various movies such as *A Few Good Men* or *My Cousin Vinny* that show various legal situations and the

Timothy D. Christ, M.B.A.

expert witnesses that testified in those matters. I romanticized the job. We became "the guys" who could figure it out. The adjusters didn't know what happened, the homeowners didn't know what happened, so they called us and we became their Superman. We flew in to help. However, I recognized my severe limitations because I didn't have sufficient knowledge. That started my journey to develop both myself and others into world-class forensic engineers.

At a very basic level, traditional economic theory is very important in this business, namely the "cost-benefit analysis." If I spend $10,000 of your money to give you a $500 expert opinion and solution, you are not going to be happy with me. Conversely, if I give you a $1 million expert opinion that saves you $500 million, then you will be very happy with my work. I say that because a very basic premise of forensic engineering is this: To arrive at the TRUTH in as expedient and cost-effective manner as possible.

Here is a quintessential claim scenario:

A family pulls up at their home and there is a line of wet concrete from their garage door out to the street. What happened?

Becoming an Expert: The Business of Forensic Engineering

The insurance adjuster decrees, go forth and determine the source of the water damage. The engineer never asks, you mean the water running from below the garage door, or any water damage at the property that I can identify?

This is the first complication to a claim scenario. The adjuster is talking strictly about the "loss scenario" that has been reported. What if there is other damage to the home that "might" be covered under a property insurance policy? Some purists will say that since it hasn't been reported it doesn't matter. During most catastrophic events, the adjusters will say, yes, the entire residence, give me a full report. During single-loss events, they generally limit the scope of the investigation to that particular loss reported. It is very important to document, on both the assignment sheet as well as the report, which type of inspection was requested. How many times have you been to a home that also has a shower pan leak, a roof leak, or an air handler leak they didn't know about, or didn't think to report?

Good forensic engineers do an initial, complete exterior walk-around of the home. Are there any other signs of water damage/intrusion or other types of damage present to the structure, or is it simply isolated to the area in front of the garage door? Secondly, they draw up a floor plan of the residence. If it is a limited scope investigation, they will draw the garage, adjoining rooms, and then simply put an outer perimeter for the remainder of the residence.

They enter the garage and discover a trail of water running along the wall, which appears to originate near the water softener system. However, the water heaters are right there as well as two windows on the wall where the water also ran. There is a shower directly on the other side of the wall in a bathroom, a toilet on that common wall, the air handler units directly above the area in the attic, and various plumbing vent penetrations through the roof close by.

What are the engineer's options at this point?

1. Strictly visual inspection of the garage, $250/hour, likely a minimum 1-hour inspection. Total cost likely $1,200-1,500.

2. Slighter longer inspection of both the garage and the attic directly above, $250/hour, likely a 1.5-2-hour inspection. Total cost now $1,500-1,800.

3. Use moisture meters to measure water content in walls, baseboards, carpet tack boards, and

other. $250/hour and add another 30 min-1 hour. Total cost now $1,800-2,100.

4. Full plumbing test of the home and equipment. This would require scheduling on a different day, return trip, and plumber cost. Total cost now $4,600.

5. HVAC analysis. Same thing as plumber above, total cost is now $5,000.

6. Destructive inspection, cutting open walls and other areas to inspect for damage. This requires hiring a contractor, because engineers don't actually cut things open. Total cost now $10,000.

7. Spray testing of the windows in accordance with ASTM E1105. This would require a technician or another engineer, spray rack, etc., total cost now $20,000.

8. Thermography with thermal imaging camera to show areas of "hidden water damage." These cameras cost up to $75,000, so this is generally billed as an individual line item, as well as an "accredited thermal imaging person" generally another engineer. Total cost now $30,000.

9. Animation/Modeling to show leaks from possible sources and model how the leak from that source would act. This requires extensive measurements, video, etc. Total cost now $55,000+.

10. If we identify subrogation potential, then we likely need a Mechanical Engineer instead of the Civil/Structural one currently performing the investigation. Whoops, that also means we should involve legal counsel! Thankfully they work on a contingent % of any recovery but the carrier will cover their actual expenses. Total cost now $65,000.

11. If we identify multiple causes of damage and several of which "might" be covered, then we should retain coverage counsel to get a policy language and case law opinion. Total cost now $85,000.

Total damage to home: $9,800. Total investigation cost: $85,000. Value provided in engineer's mind: priceless. Value provided in adjuster's mind: #&$@*! That is my argument for the cost-benefit analysis, and you can never lose sight of that when you want to be an excellent forensic engineer. This made perfect sense to the "business part" of my brain and became part of my passion.

Becoming an Expert: The Business of Forensic Engineering

The second part of my passion became being the person that "always gets it right." I am a purist in that sense of the word. I don't care what, why, or how something was caused, but I definitely wanted to be 100% correct every time any opinion ever came out of my mouth. This caused me to do three things that are extremely important to doing forensic investigation properly:

1. To achieve a greater level of understanding of any relevant facts surrounding any particular claim, in order to determine their particular "potential" influence in what project I am currently dealing with

2. To not care about who ultimately will pay what, but to focus my energy on being the guy that gives a technically correct answer all the time, even when it is not in the supposed "financial best interest" of my client.

3. To provide a world-class level of communication to my clients so that they understand what has to be done in order for me to answer their questions (read, time & budget)

Chapter 2:

UNDERSTANDING THE INSURANCE BUSINESS MODEL

When you are in a professional service business, prospects have to know, like, and trust you. There is a popular quote "They'll never care how much you know, until they know how much you care." One way to prove to them how much you care about them is to let them know that you really understand their business. They do care how much you know about your product or service, but what they are REALLY interested in knowing, is how well do you understand their business and what sort of impact can your company provide for them.

From a high level, the insurance business model is very simple.

The broker side is the revenue generation piece of the business. These are all the folks involved in selling the insurance policies to consumers and businesses. If you have ever attended a Risk Insurance Management Society (RIMS) Annual Conference, then you understand what I am talking about. There will be over 10,000 people in attendance. All the major insurers spend a lot of money on large exhibit hall booth spaces. Each large insurer throws some very nice after-hours events, such as ACE having the popular band One Republic play one year. When we were in San Diego, Zurich rented catamarans with the Zurich logo on the side of the sail and took people out cruising around the bay. This is where the insurers "wine and dine" the broker community so that the brokers will bring a lot of business to particular insurers. There are efforts to cut out the brokers from certain pieces of business, using a direct-to-consumer sales model, that is much less expensive than having to pay broker commission for every policy written.

The corporate piece has a dual-role. They manage the investments (i.e. premium dollars collected) and generally make a little bit of money from those activities. However, that is generally only a few percentage points (%) in comparison to the Gross Revenue of the entire company. The remainder of the corporate piece is an expense, including their risk management, which includes buying re-insurance to insure their risk.

The claims function is purely an expense side of the business. For most insurers, they have a combined ratio of 90%+. What that means is that after ALL expenses have been paid, for every $100 collected in premium, they will retain $10 or less as Net Income. A quick example in the auto claims world is the below chart:

Becoming an Expert: The Business of Forensic Engineering

Net Business Results for Top US Personal Insurers				
Insurer	Loss Ratio	Loss Adjustment Expense Ratio	Expense Ratio	Combined Ratio
State Farm	64.1%	16.8%	26.0%	106.9%
Geico	67.8%	10.6%	15.3%	93.7%
Allstate	57.5%	13.3%	27.7%	98.4%
Progressive	62.9%	10.6%	21.0%	94.6%

First, we will briefly explain the expense ratio column, since we won't spend much time there. This includes the commission payments to the brokers for bringing the business to the company, as well as the "corporate overhead" costs.

The loss ratio refers to the amount of money paid out in claims. State Farm, for every $100 they collected in premiums, paid out $64.10 in indemnity payments. The claims side of their business cost them another $16.80, the corporate side of their business cost them another $26.00, and so for this particular example they spent $106.90 for every $100 they brought in. Recall the recent article where State Farm lost $7 billion? Technically, they had an underwriting loss of $7 billion. The overall annual Net Income was still a positive $400 million. Since State Farm is a mutual company, it does not act like Congress where this type of behavior is acceptable. They would make some immediate changes for the next year in an attempt to get that combined ratio down. This is why you hear about rate increases. One thing interesting to note, since State Farm is by far the largest personal lines property insurer, they use money generated from their investment income to offset their auto insurance losses. They will purposely write auto business knowing they are going to lose money for several reasons:

1. Every single person that drives in America is required to have car insurance

2. Auto insurance provides great (and predictable) cash flow since most people pay the bill monthly

3. It acts like a "loss leader" for the insurer to get the person's homeowners policy, a life insurance policy, 2nd vehicle when that person gets married, etc., etc., which they do make money on

4. The more insurance policies that you have with one carrier, the higher the client retention rate for that carrier

Geico shows a combined ratio of $93.70, so that means that Geico had a Net Profit of $6.30. Since claims is purely an "expense" from an insurer standpoint, the annual conferences, such as Property Loss Research Bureau (PLRB), Loss Executives Association (LEA), and others are much less extravagant. The major insurers will send their people for the education and networking, but they will not invest a ton of money into entertainment. For that, enter the service providers. A company like BELFOR Property Restoration, which makes $100 million annually just from one major carrier, will typically throw some nice parties. I recall a BELFOR party in Nashville several years ago where Sheldon Beldon dressed up like he did during Undercover Boss. BELFOR had rented a large ballroom there at the Opryland Hotel, had a large ice sculpture on the buffet table surrounded by shrimp and hors d'oeuvres, and they had a cover band playing music.

There are two sides to the claims function, indemnity payments and claim expenses. These have an inverse relationship.

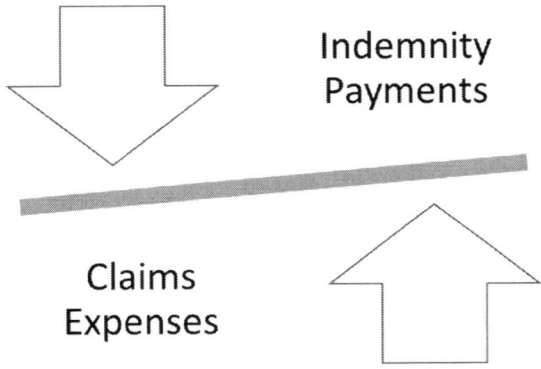

Since we have already established that we have a "fixed amount" of money (i.e. $100 in premium payments), the C-suite in an insurance company measures the rest of the company by how well they manage their part of the pie. So, for the Geico SVP of Claims, his responsibility is to manage both the $67.80 in indemnity payments and the $10.60 in loss adjustment expenses. In a given year, the SVP's big picture target number is $78.40. He will be paid a bonus for every penny that he is able to come in under that number. Conversely, if he ends up spending over that amount, then most likely he is not making any bonus that year and might even be at risk of losing his job. He will incentivize his entire organization to try to get that number down as low as possible, because he understands that for every penny below, it makes him that much more valuable in the eyes of the Board. From our chart above, he has two major theories that he can operate from:

1. Focus on Claims Expenses, or

2. Focus on Indemnity Payments

Many claims professionals, and even the general public, would at first review, say that indemnity payments are "fairly fixed." If you get into a car wreck and your car has $1,200 worth of damage, they simply write you a check for $1,200 minus your deductible (say $500), so their indemnity expenses on your claim were $700, right? That is true, but there are a myriad of factors that can influence that number, such as:

·   What if the collision was someone else's fault? My insurer still paid me the $700 but now they have the opportunity, through a subrogation action, to go collect the $1,200 from the other driver's insurance carrier (unless that driver is either uninsured or underinsured or if the accident occurs in a "No-Fault" state, such as Michigan)

·   What if my car had previous damage to the same area, and so my insurer really only owes for the damage from this particular claim?

·   What if I staged the accident so I could get a check from my carrier?

·   If I take my car to three different body shops, I'll get three different quotes, $1,200, $1,000, and $950. Which one would the insurer most like me to take my car to?

·   What if there are some other policy considerations, such as depreciation, actual cash value instead of replacement cost, rental car costs while my vehicle is in the shop, etc.

In a similar manner, there are a number of options on the claims expenses side as well (a few named for explanation purposes):

- Downsize claims operations

- Reduce claims operations expenses such as letting people work virtually from home instead of paying for large, nice office spaces

- Finding ways to streamline the claims process

- Conduct reverse-bidding wars between your service providers getting them to bid against each other for your work

- Setting up alternative claims handling processes, such as in-house counsel and/or staff counsel vs. outside counsel

- Bundling claims files toward a smaller number of service providers to get a lower dollar cost per claim but provide a larger gross revenue to the individual service provider

Once you get into larger auto loss scenarios, especially anything involving bodily injury, larger property loss scenarios, worker's compensation claims, and other, things can get complex in a hurry. In summary, the idea that indemnity payments are fairly fixed is a fallacy. In my past experience, we would document the initial claimed amount and then compare that to our recommendations for payment. The average was a 22% savings, so at least in this example, as a service provider, I have the ability to influence your indemnity payments by 22%.

Of course, I don't work for free, so that is the other side of the teeter-totter, claims expenses. Claims expenses also include all the costs involved in maintaining the claims organization; all their salaries, benefits, office space, gyms, cafeterias, corporate cars, first-class travel, etc. I recall a Claim Executive from a major insurer a few years ago was reported to have the 4th largest annual travel expense account for anyone in the company. He was very quickly counseled that he needed to manage differently because they could save a lot of money just on his travel expenses. No one questions the brokers' travel expenses because they are on the revenue generation side. That next year, he did not travel nearly as much.

Timothy D. Christ, M.B.A.

For service providers, claims expenses are our fees for investigating and managing claim files. World-class service providers do a lot of work up front, in order to manage expectations and ensure great results. If there is claim exposure of only $10,000, I recognize that insurance companies typically only want to invest 5-20% of that into claims investigation costs. So, when presented with a $10,000 potential claim and fact pattern, I review it, and based on my experience will provide an initial determination of what I would need to do to investigate it, how much it would cost, and what the likely outcomes are as a result of that work. If I feel there is a 50% chance or less of me arriving at an complete determination, then I want to let them know that up front. If I know that a particular type of investigation is required but would cost $4,000, then I want them to know that up front. As a service provider, I want to turn down the projects that are not cost-effective and would likely damage my reputation with the company. Guaranteed, no matter how much documentation that I provide up front, if I take on 100 claim files of $10,000 each and bill $5,000 on each of them, the likelihood of me continuing to get work from that company is pretty slim.

My job is to find win-win situations where my experience and expertise can really be valuable, such as a claim for $500 million dollars where my team was able to save $150 million, and our fees were only $2.6 million. That is an easily justifiable return-on-investment. Doing that type of work guarantees repeat business.

Since many of these companies are publicly traded, you can get on their website, read their 10-K's (Annual Reports) and find out all this above information as well as what their overall strategies are going forward. Then, when you meet with an insurance prospect, in light of knowing this above information, you can ask some intelligent questions:

·   How did your department perform to plan last year?

·   What are the biggest challenges that you are facing this next year?

·   What are the largest opportunities that you have this next year?

·   If I showed you some documentation that I have been able to save on average 22% on indemnity payments, would that be of interest to you?

- What is your view of how to better manage your claims expenses, especially with regard to your service providers?

- How large is your need for my product or service? How many claims files per year and/or how much money do you spend on external claim investigations?

- Who are you currently using as a service provider?

- What do you like best about what they do?

- Is there anything that you wish they would do better?

- If you could wave a magic wand over your investigation process, what would you change and why?

- If you decided to send some claim files to another service provider this year, what would they need to show you at the end of the year for you to determine if their work had been valuable to you?

Asking these types of intelligent questions to initiate a very honest and, potentially, very valuable conversation with your insurance prospect is a great way to build the "know, like, and trust" that will ultimately result in you building your business.

Chapter 3:

UNDERSTANDING THE INSURANCE CLAIMS PROCESS

For professional service providers, it is imperative to understand how your prospect's process works in order to explain to them how your particular product/service provides the most value to them. I'll highlight two scenarios of how insurers handle claims investigations:

Scenario #1:

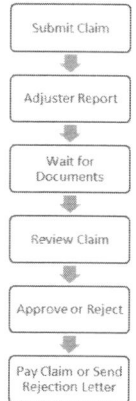

Becoming an Expert: The Business of Forensic Engineering

Scenario #2:

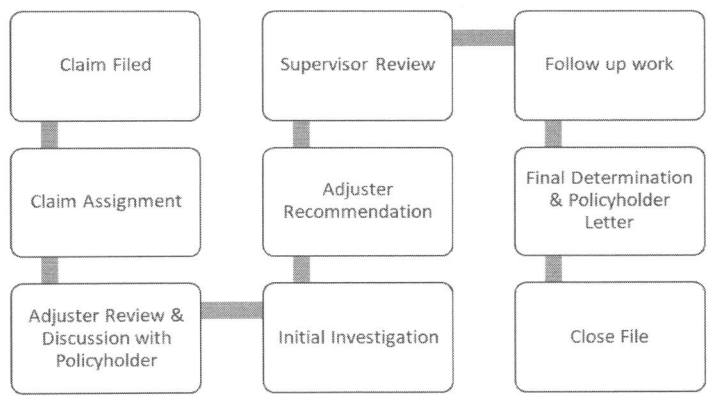

If you ask any adjuster how many steps is their process, virtually none of them will be able to tell you a specific number. Why? They will say each claim is unique. That is absolutely true, but the fundamental principles we show above, which is generally 5-9 steps.

The absolute shortest potential claim is one step. If the insured never files a "proper" notice of claim, then the insurer has no duty to respond. Depending on your jurisdiction, this has been debated at length and I'll leave it to the lawyers to explain what constitutes proper notice.

The second shortest potential claim process is two steps. A claim is filed, but there is not a policy in place during the date of the event. Most carriers issue an immediate denial of coverage for obvious reasons. However, I have been involved in a number of situations where the date of loss is a key factor, especially when you have AIG one year on a policy followed by Zurich the next year, then a loss happens within a day or two of the window when the policy changes hands. Who is liable? In a construction damage claim, for example in Texas, you have a 10-year statute of repose. So, if there is a design defect but damage doesn't manifest itself for 11.5 years, then there is generally a bar against a suit against the design professional.

A key issue to understand for service providers is the claim assignment step. In some insurers, if certain pieces of information are entered into the electronic claim system, such as "fire loss," then some carriers immediately assign that claim to a subrogation and/or Special Investigation Unit (SIU) claims handler. That person reviews the claim information for potential subrogation and/or fraud opportunity, and then reports back. If there is no subrogation or fraud potential, then the claim file gets kicked back to a 1st party adjuster. For some carriers, if the dollar value claimed is below a certain dollar amount and/or meets other certain criteria, such as $1,000, then it is directly sent to a "fast track unit." This is very common in the auto claims world for any collision that doesn't involve litigation or bodily injury but does have property damage. An Auto Property Damage (APD) adjuster is assigned. This happens in the property claims world as well. If a claim is above a certain threshold, say $100,000, then it is automatically assigned to the large loss unit.

Step 3 is where a number of errors are made in the claim adjustment process. The adjuster has competing priorities: investigate the claim thoroughly, make sure that if we owe it we pay it vs. close the claim file as quickly as possible. It's really not their fault, because an auto adjuster is likely to have an open diary of 250+ open claim files. So, you are just one of 250. Also, if you over-spend expenses on the investigation of the claim, then we will likely find another adjusting firm that will do the same work for less. The best analogy I ever heard is that the claim adjustment process is like a speeding train; if you slow it down for just about any reason, you get run over.

A key issue for adjusters is to set the loss reserve as soon as possible. This is the amount set aside to settle the claim. Improper reserving significantly disrupts actuarial tables, financial forecasting, and preparation of the annual financial statements.

Step 4 is the first real investigation. Sometimes that is the adjuster actually visiting the loss site, or, in other instances, the adjuster simply waits and relies on submitted information. Some of the best adjusters that I know have conducted an excellent initial call with the insured and based on what the circumstances are, have invited me or one of my technical staff to accompany them on the initial investigation.

A technical investigation of any insurance claim can involve (up to) seven items:

1. Determination of the area of origin

2. Determination of the cause of the incident

3. Determination of the extent of damage as a result of the incident

4. Determination of the possibility for various contributory factors (read subrogation or shared liability depending on policy and contract wording)

5. Options for repair vs. replacement

6. Loss Mitigation

7. Likelihood of Resulting Litigation, First Party or Subrogation

Step 5 is where it can get really interesting. On many occasions, insurers will send an external adjuster to do a causal and scope of damage analysis, but will reserve policy determination to be done by an internal adjuster. Some carriers allow the external adjuster to project manage the entire claim; so, this is a key point to discuss with prospects; how the claims are handled at this point and who has decision-making authority. Some external Third-Party Administrators (TPA's), especially those writing Surplus & Excess policies through a London underwriter, will have say

$25,000 in authority prior to having to submit a claim file for additional review.

Step 6 is why it is crucial to develop great relationships throughout a claims organization. If the adjuster loves you but the supervisor plays golf weekly with your competitor, then you are out of luck. Going back to Chapter 2 about the Insurance Business Model and how the SVP of Claims manages his piece of the pie, there are multiple authorization levels within a claims organization to ensure that no particular claim file ever "runs off the reservation." A good friend of mine in a large regional carrier several years ago was their "go to" claims adjuster for any potentially contentious file, because in 4+ years he had never had an excess judgement. That is great for his boss, the VP of Claims for that department, meaning he made bonus every year, but if you ask the question, "did you only pay exactly what you really owed under the policy," then they would bring up the cost/benefit analysis of closing a claim file quickly vs. complete investigation.

Step 7 is never a popular step in any claims organization, but it is recognized as an unfortunate reality. That is an investigation by outside parties, third-party service providers. However, once you save them several thousand, several hundred thousand, or several million, then they tend to warm up to you. Of course, some carriers have attempted to "commoditize" this service, by setting up a panel of experts and for one particular type of claim, simply put all the vendors on a revolving wheel where each vendor gets the 8th claim file.

Step 8 can occur within 30 days of a claim filing and it can be delivered 2 years or more after the filing date. This is the summary letter in which the adjuster puts everything together and delivers the great news to the insured; I'm paying your claim in its entirety, or, really bad news; for x,y,z reasons, your claim for $200 million is being denied, or we have found coverage for only $78,000. However, we really value you as a client and look forward to serving your needs in the future.

Step 9 is a much ignored, yet highly important step in the process. It is when the adjuster actually documents the file in the claims system as closed. This is important for when they run reports of how many open claims, average days open, etc. Unfortunately for the adjuster, if they close a file, and then the insured submits an additional damage claim or other situation, then the file is re-opened and worked all over again. Insurers also conduct "claim audits" of closed files to see how well or how poorly they performed against their internal "quality standard." Some external adjusters know that too many "re-opens" results in them losing claims volume from a carrier. With that in mind, would it make more sense to over-pay a claim by $500 or $1,000 if you figured the likelihood of a re-open would be diminished by 80%? Hence, we talk in great detail about indemnity payments and their validity. That also has to be balanced by the "open claim cost" per day, to provide justification for a slight overpayment in order to achieve a faster resolution.

Case Study

Liberty Mutual (LM) has been testing some software for their Auto Property Damage (APD) claims. These claims are pretty straight-forward, do not involve any bodily injury, and liability has been accepted by the insured. Basically, it is an event where the insured got in a wreck and admits it. Since they have paid for collision coverage, Liberty Mutual will repair their car. With this new software program, the insured takes pictures of his car and damaged areas, and submits them to LM. Within a couple minutes an estimate is generated, without any human intervention, and an offer is made to the insured. When they tested this in Beta, they intentionally offered 8-12% more than the actual repair cost because they wanted to incentivize the insured to accept the offer, so they could test this new program. The various value pieces to understand here are:

1. How much did LM save by not involving any claims adjusters in the process?
2. How much did LM save in reserve allocation?
3. With any claim, there can be a "frictional element" which can translate to customer dissatisfaction and customer turnover. Anything that speeds up the claims process and is seen as "collaborative" with the insured is a good thing. In this case, the friction is reduced, thereby providing a better claims experience, which can result in positive reviews, customer loyalty, etc. How much is that worth?
4. A small percentage of even APD claims can go to litigation, so what is the resultant savings of both fewer claims going to litigation? Another way to think about this is the savings of ALL of the downstream costs involved in longer claims cycles.
5. What other savings elements for LM can you think of?

Once you understand their process, then you can ask some intelligent questions, such as:

- What is your process?

- At what point do you typically involve service providers?

- How do you determine budgets for what your service providers do?

- Who makes the decisions on whom to involve?

- To what extent do you involve service providers? (read limited scopes of work)

- How often do you involve a service provider, even prior to actual assignment, to provide some consulting to you on options?

- What do you feel is the biggest benefit from your service providers?

- What do you feel is the biggest challenge regarding your claims process that your organization faces?

- Has your process changed or evolved over the last 5-10 years?

- Are you using new technology in your process, and if so, what type?

- What sort of accountability do you perform on your service providers?

- What would you like to see from a service provider that would cause you to recommend them on a larger majority of your claim files?

For the lawyers reading this, before you get upset about the additional steps in evaluating a coverage issue or providing a defense of a lawsuit, read Chapter 18 that covers in detail the additional steps and opportunities during the litigation process.

Chapter 4:

THE VARIOUS TYPES OF CLAIMS

From an industry perspective, insurance carriers divide themselves into two major categories: Life & Health (L&H) also known as Accident & Health (A&H) and Property & Casualty (P&C). 99.9% of the forensic engineering business is in the P&C world, although I did have a very unique life insurance case one time. Allow me to briefly digress.

An inherent fear that everyone has, joking or real, is that immediately upon them purchasing a large life insurance policy their spouse begins to look at them with a different eye. Should I ask my spouse to buckle up? Should I warn them about that bus coming? Should I encourage their risky behavior? Hopefully that made you laugh, but unfortunately the origins of this story are much more perverse…

Becoming an Expert: The Business of Forensic Engineering

I was in Monterrey, Mexico in 2004 meeting with potential clients from insurance carriers. I was meeting with a Mexican "Juridico" which simply means staff attorney for one of the largest national insurance carriers in Mexico, and as we were discussing what my firm did in Spanish, he asked me, so you do "forensics," right? I said yes, so he said hold on a minute. He left the room, and brought back some photographs of a life insurance claim with which he was dealing with. A guy had gotten divorced, married his secretary, bought a $2.5 million (USD) life insurance policy on her, and then 10 days later she "slips, falls, and dies" in the bathroom. The husband filed a claim to obtain the payout. The medical examiner's report listed the cause of death as "accidental," but obviously the carriers were suspicious.

We reviewed the information, and I said, absolutely that is something with which we can assist with. I just happen to have a Biomechanical Engineer that speaks Spanish, and has evaluated the cause and origin and extent of injury to a number of claimants.

For those not familiar with Biomechanical Engineers, they evaluate the way in which people get injured and the extent of the injuries themselves. A classic example is the low-speed car wreck. You rear-end someone at say, 3 MPH or less, and they claim a serious back injury. You say, "There is no way that I hurt their back." A Biomechanical Engineer will be doing the scientific analysis of whether your theory or their claim is more likely. They will evaluate the forces in the impact, whether or not the seat position or action of the vehicle had any influence in the incident. If the claimant is over 40, it is very likely they already had "back problems" and the collision may have "exacerbated" their injury. So, if they do have a ruptured or bulging disc, should your insurance company pay for it? That is a separate discussion.

We were retained. He went to the house in Monterrey, took detailed measurements of the bathroom, the sink height, the space around the toilet, the shower stall, etc. We built a 3D model of the bathroom, and then began comparing the bruising and marks on the body from the autopsy report, to the bathroom to identify how they may have been inflicted. There were parallel marks on her back which only matched up with the doorframe, where, we testified to later, indicated that she was slammed up against that surface. There were multiple contusions on her head, which led us to determine that her head was bashed against the toilet.

Becoming an Expert: The Business of Forensic Engineering

Another crucial piece of evidence was that the shower curtain covered her body when the paramedics arrived. Testimony from the husband stated that she was taking a shower. Had she fallen out of the shower into the bathroom, she would have ripped the curtain from the shower and fallen on it, thereby having it underneath her body as opposed to on top of her. That is why your Forensic Engineers say that we are CSI, but for real!

The case actually went to trial in Monterrey's court! The Biomechanical expert testified. The insurance carriers' denial of coverage was upheld. The most gratifying part was that upon conclusion of the civil case, the Governor of Nuevo Leon re-opened the criminal investigation into the husband and arrested him. The Nuevo Leon's local newspaper reported the entire trial and ultimate outcome. Even now, when I talk with insurance people in Mexico, they remember that case. Justice was served! When you are part of a huge win and public notoriety like that, it gets in your blood and you want to go out and do it again!

Back to the A&H vs. P&C discussion. A&H includes: medical, dental, vision, accidental death & dismemberment, life, short-term disability, and long-term disability. P&C includes the following:

1. Property – is coverage for a piece of property, be it a structure, automobile, or other. Property is also commonly called "fire insurance" even though a typical fire insurance policy would also cover some types of water damage to a structure, such as a rupture in a plumbing pipe, a discharge of water from your air conditioning system, or other. Not to confuse you more, but it is also commonly referred to as 1st party coverage, meaning that it is coverage that you the owner bought to cover assets that you own.
2. Casualty – is liability insurance related to when you, your employees, and/or one of your assets causes damage to another. Casualty is generally thought of in terms of worker's compensation, liability insurance such as commercial general liability, or other. Casualty is also known as 3rd party coverage because it is coverage that you as an owner bought to pay someone else in the event that you somehow harm them.

Each insurance carrier will have a different business set up to handle these various types of policies, and more importantly, the claims process. An adjuster that handles residential property losses does not generally handle commercial property losses, automobile damage claims, or other.

In the Forensic Engineering world, we group them this way:

A. Residential property claims
    a. Residential Small loss claims – typically $25,000 and less
    b. Residential Large Loss Claims – anything $25k+
B. Commercial property claims
    a. Small commercial – typically under $250,000 in claim
    b. Mid-size commercial – typically $250k-$5 million
    c. Large commercial – anything larger than $5 million
C. Boiler & Machinery claims – these are claims that specifically relate to pieces of equipment within a structure that may have influenced a loss, for example, a boiler that explodes and causes the building to collapse. Sometimes the equipment within a structure is too expensive to cover under just a traditional property policy, and so the 1st party property insurer will tender the "equipment coverage" to a 3rd party insurer

to spread the risk. The most famous carrier is Hartford Steam Boiler (HSB), now owned by Munich Re.
D. Commercial General Liability – is divided into 3 parts:
    a. Liability insurance to cover either bodily injury or property damage that you inflict on someone else, such as in construction defect cases where an HVAC contractor damages the roof of a building while installing the HVAC system. This coverage typically also covers some "product-related" defects, although there is separate Product Liability Insurance that can be purchased.
    b. Coverage B, also known as advertising injury coverage, is coverage for slander/libel and is where some insureds that experienced early cyber claims tried to extract coverage from their insurer
    c. Worker's compensation coverage
E. Commercial Auto – is both property and liability coverage for corporate and commercial vehicles, such as delivery trucks and 18-wheelers

F. Product Liability claims – has already been discussed above
G. Environmental Liability claims – there are special policies related to the potential to cause environmental harm and/or damage, and these coverages are typically excluded from the normal property or liability policy.
H. Error & Omission policies – these are known as "professional lines" policies because they mean that someone within your organization operated in a negligent manner and caused harm to someone else. An easy example would be a structural engineer that designs a building and then that building collapses because the engineer didn't design the structural supports to carry sufficient loads. Since that is a "design defect" and a failure of "due care given the nature of his profession" that would be covered under an E&O policy
I. Directors and Officers claims – these are policies that provide coverage when a Board of Directors or other Management team members do something that causes harm to either their organization or others.
J. Fidelity claims – also known as "fidelity bond coverage" these are claims related to fraudulent acts of individuals, such as if your employee

decides to send confidential information to a 3rd party and you suffer damages to your business

K. Cyber claims – these are claims related to errors and omissions, media liability, network security, and privacy.

L. Energy Claims – these are claims related specifically to the energy industry, be it upstream, midstream, or downstream. There are some unique policies and coverages in the Energy industry that are key to understand if you want to play in that space.

M. Marine claims – these are claims related specifically to the maritime industry, with unique names for coverages such as hull, cargo, or freight.

Chapter 5:

THE SCIENTIFIC METHOD

We all learned in our grade school science class the Scientific Method.

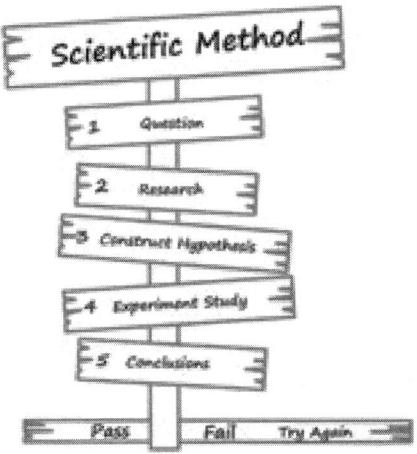

This is the foundation of the Forensic Engineering process. This is the roadmap that guides all decision-making. Step 1 is to state the question. In the insurance claims world, the question is generally: How and why did (insert incident here)

happen? Depending on the nature of the incident and the types of policies in play, it is sometimes possible to have a very limited question, such as:

1. Our policy period starts on July 1st, so we need to understand if the plumbing leak started on or after July 1st. If it started before, we are not liable for it, or
2. Our policy only provides coverage for damage to "other property" (which is very common in construction defect policies) so if my roof is defective but it has not caused interior water damage or any property damage to other building components except the roof, then there is no coverage available.

Step 2 is research. This is the investigation into the incident where forensic engineers start to gather the facts, evidence, witness testimony, and other information pertaining to the incident. Step 3 is construct hypotheses. A basic tenet of forensic engineering is to NOT pre-determine the outcome. The question for the engineers is, what is the mechanism of failure? What person, performance, system, or process (or a combination thereof) failed in some form or fashion and caused this incident? What process deviated from a known standard or recommendation, such as Standard Operating

Procedures, Occupational Health & Safety Administration (OSHA) guidelines or industry best practices?

We read articles about it all the time where an engineer stated "there is no hail damage to that roof," and then a contractor's report shows a large number of hail impressions to the roof. How could an engineer be so blind? In Chapters 7-13, we'll detail individual case studies that show either engineering failures or other failures. The very basic example early in the book related to the water claim from the garage showed us the water "might" have come from any number of sources:

1. Garage windows
2. Water softener
3. One of two water heaters
4. Shower pan and/or shower plumbing
5. Toilet and/or toilet plumbing
6. Overhead HVAC unit
7. Roof leak
8. Other?

The important part, especially if you ultimately testify in court, is to be able to demonstrate that you at least considered ALL possible causes of the damage before you made a determination. Otherwise, you failed to use the scientific method properly and therefore your testimony is unreliable.

Step 4 is Experiment and Study. In a few of our past cases, it required us to conduct some experiments and study those results in order to determine which results most closely matched the evidence that was presented by this particular claim. Once you have been able to conclusively rule out ALL other potential causes, the scientific method allows you to say with certainty, this (insert cause here) caused the damage exhibited in the (insert incident here). In Chapter 18 we'll touch in more detail some court opinions regarding the scientific method and how expert witnesses use that process to arrive at opinions.

Step 5 is to analyze the data and make conclusions. This is where some engineers get hung up and where experience comes in. For example, if there are two possible causes, but one is much more likely than the other, then the engineer is frequently called upon to make the judgment call and support it. If he has had 10 or 100 prior cases that are similar, then he can testify, in 100 cases like this I have seen, it has only been proven that Option A happened in 10 of the cases, and Option B occurred in 90 or 95.

Timothy D. Christ, M.B.A.

Chapter 6:

DIFFERENCES IN VARIOUS SERVICE PROVIDERS

I'll write a hypothetical letter to an Insurance Company SVP of Claims.

Dear Sir:

If you ask anyone in the insurance industry about the best way to conduct business, they'll all answer the same way "We do business with those we like, know, and trust." Relationships are key. However, how do you get some true "insight" into the operations of a service provider? Here are some questions you might consider asking (WARNING: Some service providers may be unprepared or really upset to answer these questions. Thankfully, there is a reason for that).

Most of us have filled out the Request for Qualifications and/or Request for Proposals issued by your Procurement Department. Ask any service provider and I guarantee you they will say, the best RFP's/RFQ's they have ever read are the ones that had "Expert Assistance" in crafting the request.

What you really want to figure out is which vendor is the game-changer for a particular piece of your business. It's like assembling a puzzle. You understand what your puzzle looks like at the end of the day, and it is your job to figure out which vendors can streamline/add efficiencies/provide greater value/cost less to your puzzle assembly process. For example, a recent example with one carrier occurred where they had decided to use Rimkus and EFI for all their fire investigation work across the country. After a couple months of being on this "new program," they found the work load was too much for just these two companies and have now added Unified Investigations as an approved vendor. This is really silly because this could have easily been determined during the RFP and contracting stages.

#1. What is your UNIQUE VALUE PROPOSITION for our firm? In order for them to provide that information to you, you will likely have to allow them to conduct an analysis/discovery process to understand your current systems, processes, procedures, and infrastructure. How are they faster/better/cheaper in a meaningful and demonstrable way? There are certain companies that use air conditioning technicians instead of engineers to evaluate lightning strike claims. Their reports are typically provided faster and at a cost of 1/3 to ½ of the cost of an engineer.

#2. How valuable will our business be to your firm? In other words, where will we rank in terms of priority and service with your other clients? Will we have any dedicated resources? What expectations of replies, on-site response, or other can we expect? What level of authority does that person have regarding our business, such as can they make immediate decisions without consulting others?

#3. How efficient will you be in managing our business?

When I first started conducting investigations, a residential investigation for a house of 2,000 square feet would take me 4-6 hours to complete. I would draw a floor plan (and many times, have to re-draw it, because doors, walls, or rooms wouldn't line up correctly the first time). I would conduct a room-by-room analysis, take pictures and make notes. On my early investigations, I would forget to document closely where certain things were located, so at the report-writing phase, I would have to give an approximation, instead of a specific. Ask any field adjuster and all of them will say, they occasionally have photos and they forgot where they are located. I would conduct some sampling and other testing. If I didn't immediately label it correctly, then I could mix up samples. I would conduct an interview with the homeowner, but I wouldn't always ask all the right questions. The report could take me about 8 hours to draft. It would take an hour or two for my peer report, because there would be a number of errors in it. Then I would do my re-drafting and final publishing. At $200/hour, 6 hours inspection, 10 hours report writing, and 2 hours peer review, the total cost would be $3,600.

Fast forward about six months, and I can do the same inspection in 1.5 hours. Report takes me another hour. Peer review takes about 30 minutes. $600 total cost. From the outside looking in, how do you know if it should cost $3,600 or $600? Agreed that early on our internal processes would have likely capped my billings on this file to say $2,000 or so. However, what if it is the other way as well? What if I am billing $2,000 (because I budgeted that, or because I know the market bears it) when it only took me 3 hours?

Timothy D. Christ, M.B.A.

#4a. Who are the most efficient billable staff in your company (i.e. the ones who bill their time and have the least write-offs)? This is subjective and can be manipulated, so it is a hard subject with which to get an apples-to-apples answer. However, I have seen consultants with 1-2% annual write-off rates and others with 30-40%.

#4b. Which consultants typically have the least errors in their initial reports and consequently, have the least amount of peer review time typically billed? If the service provider "caps" their peer review time at a certain amount, then this question has to be re-phrased.

#5. Of your staff, when you have a tight deadline, a pre-determined budget, and it's imperative to maintain a near perfect degree of accuracy, who is your consultant of choice? If they tell you all 100 out of 100 consultants, they are full of $#&%. Follow the 80/20 rule on this. 20% of all their consultants are "possible rock stars" in this arena.

#6. For particular lines of business, who are your "best" consultants? Do you promise to assign only those individuals to our files? As complexity increases, the requirement to have a seasoned expert increases for obvious reasons.

#7. How do you plan to use my file assignments in the training of your junior staff? We all know that new hires will get some of these files, so what is the expectation for competency, oversight, billing efficiency, and other?

#8. Will you engage in some workshop training where we assemble our respective teams and role-play the way in which our future relationship should act?

#9. Are you willing to have us "pilot-test" your services, so that we can compare them against other service providers in a similar space?

#10. What is your annual and 3-year turnover rate? This question is key, because we have all seen cases be investigated and then when it finally goes to trial the expert is with another firm, and there is always that tension of allowing the expert to gain access to his complete file, talk directly with the client, the prior firm having virtually no "control" over the work-product anymore, etc., so you'd like to minimize those circumstances as often as possible.

#11. Can we engage in quarterly or semi-annual reviews to monitor and improve our relationship? This should be a no-brainer, but many times it falls by the wayside because the key decision makers are "too busy." Worthwhile relationships take time, energy, and effort by both sides to really develop into know, like, and trust.

It is without question that the best way to evaluate them is to "see them in action." However, that is like signing up a new baseball player for your team and having him pitch the opening game instead of seeing how he does in practice first. I'm sure your insured would not appreciate having a brand-new expert "practice" on their claim file. Once you have witnessed 4-8 different investigators in their process and seen the results, you'll instinctively know which ones are better. However, when trying to roll this up into a "national or global program" the ability to have that sort of on-site analysis is severely curtailed. These questions will let you get a "peek behind the curtain" into the worlds of service providers.

What other questions have you used to gain further insight into the differences in service providers?

Chapter 7:

GREAT FIRE INVESTIGATION

There are a number of fire investigators, both nationally and abroad, that will "take the side" of what they perceive to be their client's interest. In the insurance arena, if a warehouse is occupied by two parties, and there is a fire investigator assigned to each of the tenants, it is not unusual to have the official opinion of the one saying that the fire started on the other side, and for the opinion of the other to say the exact same thing but for the other party. There was a large loss in Latin America I was involved in where two prior fire investigators actually wrote reports opining on the area of origin when neither party had been allowed inside the building!

Many fire investigators "believe" that if they can find a reason to say that it is not the "fault" of their client, then their client will appreciate them more and likely hire them again in the future. Great fire investigators arrive at the scene without any preconceived ideas. They explain to their client the steps that have to be undertaken in order to make a decision on the area of origin of the fire, not to mention the cause. There may be eyewitness testimony that says one thing, there may be physical evidence that shows something else, and there may be yet another reason (such as early clearing of the fire scene by unknown parties) that creates a difficult scene to reconstruct. The great fire investigators take ownership of all these moving parts, chart a path to investigate following the guidelines of NFPA 921 and 1033 (making sure they are following the correct version), and work to arrive at a scientifically-based conclusion. In any forensic investigation, there are no shortcuts. There are sometimes opportunities to evaluate specific "if-then" statements, and if that provides sufficient information for your client, then there are ways to go about performing that sort of "limited investigation" while not compromising the integrity of a true forensic investigation. The scope can be plainly identified with all the hypotheticals itemized, and then review the available information to see if those various hypotheticals can be conclusively ruled in or out.

Many fire investigators believe in their innate ability to determine the cause and origin of a fire simply by what we will call a cursory evaluation. I've been involved in $20 million+ USD property loss cases where an initial investigator is on-scene for 2-4 hours, performs no scene clearing, and provides an opinion on cause of the fire. Taking it one step further is for a fire investigator to have a collapsed structure where the roof is now covering the debris, and to make an initial determination without even removing the roof covering! What we also know is that the NFPA 921 manual has substantially evolved over the years. It used to be considered that the area of heaviest damage was generally the area of origin. With experience and a number of experiments, we now know that ventilation can play a large role in the fire spread and ultimately impact the extent of damage in various areas.

Arc mapping is a fairly recent phenomenon that has been introduced as a scientifically valid way to determine whether electrical cables were energized at the time of a fire, and to determine which areas of the cable failed first, thus providing some additional clues to the likely area of origin. Great fire investigators can provide a few plausible theories based upon the evidence plainly available (in many cases, witness statements), but will withhold an ultimate opinion until they have investigated to the point where they have "reasonable certainty", including discounting potential causes.

Timothy D. Christ, M.B.A.

Some fire investigators have had their hand caught in the proverbial cookie jar when they have "opined" on electrical or mechanical engineering issues. Courts are quick to dismiss this type of proffered testimony because it is clearly outside the bounds of their demonstrated competence. An Electrical Engineer should ALWAYS review the electrical system in any investigation where it may have been an issue. A Mechanical or Electrical Engineer should ALWAYS examine a piece of equipment where it may have been involved as a cause or simply a consequence of the fire.

Attention to detail separates the great ones as well. I was involved in a $100 million or so fire investigation where the initial investigator incorrectly sketched the scene. It resulted in his placing an electrical panel very close to his area of origin. When we measured and drew the scene, the actual location of the electrical panel was in excess of 30' from the area of origin. In a manufacturing facility of +/- 500,000 square feet with extensive damage, it was easy for him to make the small mistake in his drawing. That mistake, however, obviously had a tremendous impact on his ultimate opinion on the cause of the fire. How excited do you think his client was when he looked at his expert's drawing, and then compared it with ours and the photographs?

Lastly, but definitely not least, is the report. Some fire investigators have reports that are 30 pages in length discussing the plant operation, age of equipment, personnel, activities, etc. Then there is one paragraph at the bottom of the last page that says the cause of the fire was an electrical short circuit. Great fire investigators allow for pages of explanation showing the fire progression, discussing the evidence that led them back to the area of origin, explaining the dig-out activities that resulted in that location to uncover fused/charred evidence, evaluating any electrical, mechanical, or other potential ignition sources in the area, and corroborating the witness statements with the physical evidence.

Great fire investigation is both an art and a science. The great ones assume nothing and let the evidence guide the way to the determination. This can be frustrating for clients who love quick resolutions and decisions, but when hundreds of millions of dollars of property damage and business interruption is on the line, as well as the expert's professional reputation, it's better to be right than expedient.

Timothy D. Christ, M.B.A.

Chapter 8:

STRUCTURAL ENGINEERING CASES

For these next several chapters, I'm simply going to give a case study and then provide some commentary as we walk through the process. The first one is a Property Damage case. The insured, a hotel owner in Galveston, filed a property claim for hurricane damage to their property after Hurricane Ike hit Galveston. The first big issue after Ike was whether the property was damaged by the hurricane winds or by the storm water surge. This is important because there are two different policies that cover each of these. Any wind damage is covered by the traditional property policy, in this case issued by the Texas Windstorm Insurance Association. Any storm surge damage is covered by the NFIP flood policy. This was a hotel on Galveston island that experienced damage from both the wind and from the surge.

The property adjuster calls and says, "I've got a commercial property, a hotel, on Galveston that was damaged by Hurricane Ike and we need to go determine the cause and extent of damage." We head out there and find that the roof has been peeled away in places due to the high winds and the first floor of the building flooded with about 12 feet of water. Since there are two policies at play, we have to segregate the damage from the wind and the damage from the surge. Complicating the claim was the fact that there were sections of the roof that were in extreme states of disrepair and had long exhausted their useful life. So, we had to carefully delineate those areas from the areas that had been in good condition but were still damaged by the wind. There were areas to the interior of the hotel that had been damaged by other sources, including, prior plumbing leaks, old window leaks, etc. These areas as well needed to be carefully segregated by cause of loss and their applicable extent of damage. The hotel owner got a contractor to provide an initial repair estimate that was nearly $20 million. It included doing lead and asbestos abatement in a number of pipe chases throughout the facility. Our expert opinion was that the lead and/or asbestos had not been damaged in any way by the storm, so the adjuster then concluded that there was no causal link for those areas. That by itself was about $4 million. Once we fully delineated the different types of causes, their associated areas of water damage and the cost of repair, then the adjuster applied the policy, subtracted for depreciation, etc. Our estimate was about $6 million and that was being slightly generous on our part. That had been discussed with the adjuster. We are normally not asked to "take a razor's edge to our pencil" but rather to be as generous as possible, so when there is something that is considered "grey" to give it to the insured. There is a basic tenet of insurance contracts that the insurer has the upper hand when negotiating the initial policy with the insured. If a claim arises and for some reason it is not clear cut, then the decision should be in favor of the insured. However, in this case, since $6 was a long way from $20, the insured wanted to fight about it. We provided some follow up documentation, sat in on a mediation at the request of the adjuster, and then heard from him about six months later they had finally settled for about $7.5 million. To me, that is a big win. The initial claim was $20, our estimate was $6, and because the insurer wanted to save money rather than spend it on future litigation costs, agreed to put another $1.5 million on the table to make the claim settle.

Chapter 9:

CONSTRUCTION CASES

My favorite line that represents the construction industry is the movie Armageddon's Lowest Bidder line (remember where they had to send the astronauts to space to blow up a meteor that was going to crash into earth?):

Rockhound says to Harry Stamper: Hey Harry.

Harry to Rock: Yeah Rock.

Rockhound: You know we are sitting on something that has 4 million pounds of fuel, one nuclear weapon, and a thing that has 270,000 moving parts built by the lowest bidder. Makes you feel good, doesn't it?

Harry: Yeah.

Timothy D. Christ, M.B.A.

That is construction in a nutshell. There are popular statistics out there that show contractor failure rates, meaning the % of contractors that go out of business, varies between 14.6% and 29%, depending on the type of construction (trade contractors, heavy highway, nonresidential buildings, or industrial).

Another sad fact is that only 15% of General Contractors have written quality management systems. According to popular literature, the average contractor makes an average of 10% errors. The most common causes of construction defects are faulty materials, faulty workmanship, and faulty design.

The construction stages are as follows:

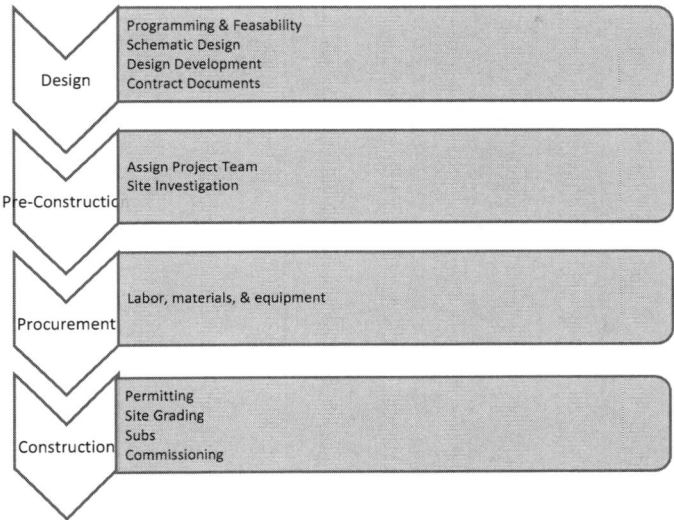

A very popular term in construction is the Critical Path Method (CPM). This is a documented series of critical steps that must be followed in order for a particular project to reach a successful conclusion. This is also typically the basis for construction delay claims, where one of the involved parties will show where the project deviated from this CPM and then what the resulting impact to their particular business was.

More specific types of common construction defects include:

- Building envelope and structure
    - Doors and windows
    - Exterior walls
    - Roofs
    - Waterproofing

- Infrastructure
    - Drainage
    - Compaction & structural
    - HVAC
    - Plumbing
    - Sound, vibration, odor, and/or code compliance deficiencies

Quality and safety go hand-in-hand to prevent construction defects. The best contractors with respect to safety performance and risk transfer also had the fewest claims.

There are five leading indicators in quality management:

1. 100% material verification – this means when materials arrive on-site they are reviewed to determine that they are in-fact the correct materials for this particular job.
2. Pre-install and first-work-in-place meetings – these are simply short "huddles" between the GC team and the subcontractors to ensure that everyone is on the same page regarding what is to happen and how. This was originally developed by the US Corps of Engineers.
3. Zero defect program – committing to resolving defects as they occur, and not simply covering them up. The goal is to complete the General Contractors scope of work with a zero punchlist at the time of substantial completion
4. Digital photography procedure – documentation of the work by the various subcontractors to ensure compliance with drawings and specifications
5. Pre-closure inspection sign-off procedure including digital photographs – this is a quality management procedure done by someone other than the subcontractor doing the work to ensure

what they have done complies with the drawings and specifications

The vast majority of construction defects involve water in some way.

On construction sites, the General Contractor is tied very closely to a deadline. Most will have liquidated damages clauses for failure to meet a deadline. This can mean tens of thousands of dollars per day that a contractor is late. Obviously, this can cause him to want to "speed along" the process if he feels that he can take care of any small problem that shouldn't cause any real damage to the project. A true forensic investigation determines "what is the root cause of this problem" not, how do we work around it?

Certificates of Merit have become legal instruments in some states where construction defect claims are prevalent. This means you have to have an Architect or Engineer write a report that states the root cause of problems found to a structure and explain how the design architect or design engineer failed to uphold their quality standard in some way that should allow one of the parties to sue the Professional Architect or Professional Engineer for negligence or gross negligence. This is a pre-requisite to filing against the

Design Professional. If a Certificate of Merit is not an attachment to the initial pleading, then the court can rule the case dismissed with prejudice.

There are some unique insurance policies associated with the construction world as well. One of the most popular ones in the last few decades has been "wrap policies" such as Owner-Controlled Insurance Programs (OCIP) or Contractor-Controlled Insurance Programs (CCIP). Texas courts and others view these types of policies as the "sole remedy." The main use for this is to control the subcontractor "workman's compensation" claims on construction sites, where a roofing contractor would get injured, but would claim that it was due to the masonry contractor's negligence, the General Contractor's negligence, or any party other than his employer. At least in Texas, an injured party is barred from suing his employer if they have workman's compensation insurance. Plaintiff's lawyers found a convenient way around this to allege fault by a third party. The insurance industry's answer to this was with these wrap policies as a way to minimize risk during this inherently risky activity called construction.

Timothy D. Christ, M.B.A.

Chapter 10:

MECHANICAL ENGINEERING CASES

We had a manufacturing facility in Mexico City that suffered a loss to one of their injection molding machines. The machine had seized up and quit working, so they filed an insurance claim. Their property policy initially responded, but when they realized that it was purely an equipment failure, they notified their Boiler & Machinery coverage company to investigate. We get the phone call that we have a large manufacturer that has suffered a mechanical breakdown of this injection molding equipment and they want us to perform a cause and origin, extent of damage, and also provide repair/replacement cost options.

We met the adjuster on the site with the insured and their maintenance team, and then we started to investigate the machine. We pulled the data from their systems that showed how long that machine had been running, at what operating temperatures, and when the last maintenance procedures had been performed on it. This particular machine was Russian in manufacture, and the plant personnel didn't have a completely translated maintenance manual into Spanish. What we found is that during their last maintenance operation they had replaced a number of bearings. These ball bearings were about the size of golf balls, and there were 24 in this particular machine. We found extreme deformation to the areas where these ball bearings were located, which indicated extreme heat buildup, and then easily understood why the machine seized up when it deformed past its operational tolerances.

We conducted metallurgical analyses on these ball bearings and we learned their hardness measure on the Mohs scale. We translated the original Russian design and operation manual into Spanish and showed them the types of bearings that had been originally installed on the unit. We showed them the types of bearings that they had purchased from a local machine supplier and their related hardness. Unfortunately, the bearings they purchased were primarily platinum in composition, which ranked about a 4. The original bearings were mostly titanium and ranked a 6. This meant that the bearings they used would fail more quickly under the normal operating temperatures and pressures of this machine.

Timothy D. Christ, M.B.A.

The boiler & machinery carrier then entered into negotiations with the insured because they had language in their policy that discussed how it was the responsibility of the insured and their staff to "properly maintain" and provide the recommended "on-going maintenance" for the equipment, and in this case, it was obvious that the insured had failed to uphold their contractual agreement.

The insured had an equipment repair company that had said the entire machine was damaged beyond repair and required full replacement at a cost of $7 million. We explained to the carrier and the insured that repairs and some machining could repair the equipment for about $1.75 million. The B&M carrier was not technically on the hook for the loss, but they settled with the insured for about $1 million because the insured had a $250,000 deductible.

Our client was happy with the outcome and therefore, so were we. In mechanical cases that deal with equipment that has failed, you have to analyze all potential causes: design, installation, operation, maintenance, and other. It was also highly valuable to the process that we used a local metallurgical facility with the proper Mexican credentials as well as internationally-recognized laboratory certifications.

That gave the insured a higher degree of confidence that we were truly "independent experts" as opposed to simply being hired guns trying to help the insurer get out of paying a valid claim.

One of the "art" pieces of the forensic engineering business is conducting the witness interviews. The goal is to extract as much information as possible, without asking questions in such a way that they "recognize" that their answer will cause their employer to be cast in a negative light, or even worse, to not receive any money. So, you have to act like Columbo in a way where you ask a series of questions but insert some random questions at various points to keep them a little off balance and simply responding honestly to you, without thinking about the consequences of their answers. Most plant maintenance workers will tell you if they run the equipment harder than it is supposed to be run, or if they had another piece of equipment go out of service a month ago, and so now have had to double production through other equipment. They are thinking in terms of process and work flows, while we are thinking in terms of cause and origin as well as ultimate liability for the incident.

Timothy D. Christ, M.B.A.

Chapter 11:

ELECTRICAL ENGINEERING CASES

We had a very famous case in Mexico regarding a backup generator. The San Antonio Spurs were set to play an exhibition game with the Minnesota Timberwolves in December 2013. This game was intended to be "the" game for the introduction and development of the National Basketball Association (NBA) in Latin America. Since there are frequent power grid fluctuations in Mexico City, the arena decided to run the backup generator all day and then throughout the game. Just before game time, smoke started pouring out of the generator room. They had to cancel the game. The following parties were put on notice: the insurance carrier for the arena, the Electrical Contractor responsible for servicing/maintaining all the electrical equipment, the manufacturer of the generator, and the subcontractor installers for some of the wiring and venting.

The first expert for the arena determined that it was a discarded cigarette that caused the fire and subsequent smoke. In Mexico this is a very common cause of loss because many people smoke. It is considered to be "a likely cause" by the general populace, and the 1st party insurer will pay the claim and not think too much about it. That satisfies the insured because they receive a claims payment. The only loser in that scenario is the 1st party property insurer because they might have had a subrogation claim against a 3rd party and recovered their costs. In this instance we found that an installation defect in the way the venting was installed, which led to an airgap, which allowed hot gases to escape, make contact with the motor surface and flash into a fire. Unfortunately, for the Primary Electrical Contractor who had subcontracted that part of the work out, his subcontractor didn't have sufficient insurance to pay the damages, so the Primary Electrical Contractor's Commercial General Liability Carrier had to step in and pay the remainder of the claim, minus the deductible, which the primary electrical contractor had to pay. However, the 1st party property insurer was thrilled by our findings.

Also, the manufacturer of the generator was thrilled to know that their generator had not "mal-functioned" in any way which also meant that they were not ultimately responsible either. This was a very large business interruption claim because they didn't end up playing that game at all over the Christmas season.

In Electrical Engineering cases, similar to Mechanical Engineering cases, you have to evaluate all the potential options: design, installation, operation, maintenance, and other. In cases where there are other experts, it is best to simply keep your mouth shut and let them take the lead. Many times, the ones with the outgoing personalities and the ones who like to "take charge" will let a lot of things come out of their mouth that you can simply document. Once you have collected all the information and come to the right conclusion, you can use that documentation to discredit their opinions at the proper time. It is almost NEVER a good idea to try to discredit another expert on a site investigation.

Only if someone is going to spoliate evidence in some form or fashion or cause irreparable damage to something important would we then interfere and provide alternative suggestions. Otherwise, we'll simply tag along, keep two eyes and ears open, and then conduct whatever additional investigation is needed at the end after the others have finished.

Timothy D. Christ, M.B.A.

Chapter 12:

PETROLEUM ENGINEERING CASES

Some Energy cases are straightforward property damage or liability cases, but then some can take a unique angle because of the type of processes going on and the types of equipment being used. Energy claims are usually classified in one of four ways:

    Upstream – means the activities centered around locating and producing oil and/or gas from the ground and getting it to the surface of the earth.

    Mid-stream – means the activities to transport the oil and/or gas between the production field and a processing facility.

Becoming an Expert: The Business of Forensic Engineering

  Downstream – means the activities involved in the processing of oil and/or natural gas in order to turn them into usable products

  Utility – means any activity to generate power, such as coal-fired power plants, natural gas power plants, etc.

There was a very large oil and gas drilling company that was drilling an offshore well in the Gulf of Mexico off the coast of Texas. They had what is known as a "Control of Well" (COW) claim, which means they lost operational control of the well they were drilling, had to incur some unforeseen costs in order to regain control of the well, and then continue with their drilling project. Essentially this particular type of policy is a "gap policy" designed to cover expenses above and beyond normal drilling operations when one of any series of events occurs that ultimately results in the operator "losing control" of the well.

Imagine sticking a large straw into a coke can and then sticking a smaller straw inside the larger one. What happens in oil drilling is in your smaller straw you send down your drilling tool and you are sending down fluid to keep your drill bit cool as well as bring debris to the surface, and so you pump fluid into the smaller straw, it goes down the straw into the coke can, and then comes back up the space between the smaller straw and the larger straw. This is also called the "interstitial space" or backside of the drilling string. If you pump 50 gallons of fluid down, you expect to receive 50 gallons back to the surface. That means that you have "good returns" and provides confirmation that you have control of your well. What happened in this case is that they were pumping fluid down, but they were not getting fluid back to the surface. That means the fluid was leaking into the coke can and going somewhere else. That is an underground blowout, and is a trigger event under a COW policy.

In these types of claims it is extremely important to document the exact time when they lost control of the well to the exact time they regained control, because the offshore platform they were using rents for $50,000/day. This was presented to us as a $12 million claim. An Energy adjuster had already been working this claim for several months but had yet to reach an agreement between the insured and the insurer. When we got involved and analyzed the sequence of events, we found that there were a few operational errors conducted by the drilling company which compounded the problem. As part of the COW policy, it describes "a standard of care" being used in these operations. Since we were able to show how and where they deviated from the "best practices" when dealing with this type of situation, we were able to reduce the claim amount from $12 to $7 million. When we further segregated all the incurred costs from the costs submitted, we found only about $4 million in "additional costs" that should have been incurred as a result of this event. The original adjuster was not really happy with our work because we made him look a little foolish in that he didn't catch that "technical error" and he professes to be a Control of Well expert. However, our insurer client was thrilled with our findings and, when presented with the information, the insured's engineering team concurred with our assessment.

Product Liability cases in the energy arena are often an excellent opportunity for subrogation. A famous example is when the blowout preventer on the Macondo Rig failed to close as designed. That was not the primary cause of the incident, however, it was a contributing factor. The main cause of the Macondo loss was the lack of a professional engineer on the rig at the time of the blowout. They were "rigging down" that rig, about to cap the well and move to another location. They were offloading fluid to another vessel, but, failed to measure the returns. So, the exact opposite of the earlier case study is what happened in Macondo. They were pumping 50 barrels down and getting 80 barrels in return. That meant the returns included a lot of oil/gas mixture from down in the well. That gas eventually made its way all the way up the drill pipe onto the rig, found a spark, and exploded. There was a severe reaction in the upstream energy community after Macondo. For example, Chevron hired some independent, 3rd party Petroleum Engineers to be a "second set of eyes" on all their active drilling wells. These guys would make $400/hour, work a 12-on, 12-off hour shift, and work 6 months a year. Per rig, you would need 4 of these guys. Each of these guys would make about $900,000/year working 6 months per year. It cost Chevron about $4 million per year per rig to run this program. However, when you look at a $1 billion-dollar rig loss like Macondo, a few million per year is a drop in the bucket.

Energy cases can be unique because there is specialized equipment and some very unique processes that occur. It's best on these types of claims, just like any other, to find a technical expert that is well-versed in the actual operations of whatever was happening at the time of the failure. However, the additional best practice is that generally this technical expert is not going to be an expert on the nuances of policy language: things like timing triggers, exclusions, limitations, extent of damage, delay periods for business interruption, or other. So, it takes someone that is well-skilled in both worlds in order to arrive at the technically accurate opinion that has completely answered all the questions that are asked by both the carrier and the insured.

Timothy D. Christ, M.B.A.

Chapter 13:

ENVIRONMENTAL ENGINEERING CASES

Environmental Engineering cases are a lot of fun because they have their own particular nuances as well. They have separate policies that deal specifically with this type of issue and they have their own causes of loss, exclusions, limitations, etc. One of the most enjoyable projects I worked on was the environmental remediation of the Sony Semiconductor plant in San Antonio, when the National Security Agency bought the building to house their Cryptologic Center.

We had been hired because a contractor had identified potential environmental contamination in the building, including asbestos and mold. We initially performed a cursory Environmental Assessment to determine if we thought there was any contamination present. We confirmed that indeed there was, and were then tasked with performing a complete Environmental Assessment. We mapped the entire facility, took a number of samples, and provided a comprehensive report on all the asbestos, mold, lead, and other heavy metals contamination that was present in the facility. Remediation Contractors were brought on to bid the job, they conducted pilot tests for cleaning, and we conducted initial clearance testing. They passed so the client contracted with one of the Remediation companies and they got to work. The first real clearance test they failed miserably primarily due to their methods and procedures of removing the contamination. Our joint client, the General Contractor based out of Maryland, then contracted with us to provide on-site oversight and management of the remediation crews. I lived on that job for 16 weeks. Every Monday morning, I showed up at 8a and every Friday afternoon I left around 5p.

They simply needed some additional training and oversight related to cleaning, ingress/egress procedures, quality control, and safety. I walked the facility with their superintendents, pointed out areas of concern, provided on-the-spot recommendations to their procedures and methods, documented the conversations, and had weekly meetings with our client to go over the progress. This is where you see all that really goes on in the contracting world. Since there were asbestos and heavy metals present, I wore a TIVEK suit, hard hat, and respirator the entire time. I found the contracting crew smoking cigarettes inside the asbestos containment on more than one occasion. It was too much trouble for them to exit through the decontamination showers to exit the building to get a smoke, so they removed their respirators and lit up right there. They had a couple additional small fails, but we completed their work in their initial timeline plus 24 days. The remediation contractor was very upset because they had a liquidated damages penalty to pay for their failure to complete the job in their allotted time frame.

However, with the daily, weekly, and monthly documentation that we had assembled, they had no maneuvering room. It was very clear that if they had assigned additional staff and additional management to the job they could have finished more quickly. However, they didn't include that in their original estimate, nor did they budget for failing any clearance tests and having to go back and re-clean the same areas twice.

Our General Contractor client was thrilled with our work. There is a popular quote in our business that if you haven't made someone extremely happy and at the same time you have really pissed someone off, then you haven't done a good job. I don't quite believe that, but in this case, it was the truth. Facts don't lie and the truth can hurt.

Timothy D. Christ, M.B.A.

Chapter 14:

VEHICLE ACCIDENT RECONSTRUCTION CASES

We had a running joke in Rimkus South Texas, Which holiday will we NOT have to go work a car wreck? Thanksgiving or Christmas? Several years in a row found us on the side of some lonely stretch of highway the day after Thanksgiving or Christmas. Vehicle Accident Reconstructions (VAR's) are neat cases to work. You've got two or more vehicles (or occasionally a single one) that somehow come together and you've got to figure out how it happened and whose fault it was. Whereas many property claims simply involve property damage, unfortunately vehicle accident claims often involve serious bodily injury and sometimes death.

Becoming an Expert: The Business of Forensic Engineering

We took a group of adjusters to Copart to do a VAR class one time. We were walking around their yard full of crashed vehicles, picking out cars at random to show different technical details related to the damage. One car had a windshield that had obviously been impacted from the passenger compartment, and right in the middle where the spiderwebbed cracks started, were long gray hairs stuck in it. Obviously some older woman's head had impacted the windshield right there and we were not aware of whether or not she survived. Many of these accident scenes will have a lot of blood on them, so they are not for the faint of heart.

Being the junior guy on these scenes, I was always the "pole man." We used a Total Station to do a digital mapping of the accident scene that would download directly into our animation program so that way we could run different scenarios. Your High School Geometry comes back to you because you start to look at angles of impact, skid marks, gouge marks, paint transfer, lines of travel, and you can start to figure out how these two cars came together. You also get to use a lot of math to do calculations related to the vehicle speed of travel, traffic signal timing, and more.

Probably our most fun VAR case was one where a Grocery 18-wheeler collided with multiple vehicles on

Timothy D. Christ, M.B.A.

I-35 near San Antonio. There was an allegation that perhaps the truck had been impacted by a dump truck and then swerved into all those other vehicles. That would be critically important from a liability perspective because then the dump truck and its insurance would be on the hook for the damage and deaths that resulted. In order to test this theory, the Grocer gave us an 18-wheeler truck and trailer. We took it to a test track in Uvalde, TX, and we tried to wreck it. We had several lead and chase vehicles, and had cameras and all sorts of equipment installed to monitor everything, but in the end, we were unable to recreate any event that would show the dump truck had any influence on the wreck. For the Grocer, that meant they were on the hook for everything.

Northwestern University has an accreditation called ACTAR, Accreditation Commission for Traffic Accident Reconstruction, and it is widely viewed as the standard by which to judge accident reconstruction consultants. Many VAR experts are former cops. Those cops will tell you that 99% of what they did was not full reconstructions. Just like in the fire world with fire marshals, the most important thing for the cop is to simply process the scene, determine if any laws were broken, and move on to the next file. Some larger police forces will have a dedicated VAR team, and those folks can be very good. However, the run of the mill Sheriff, Police Officer, or other, has taken 1 or 2 basic courses in Accident Reconstruction and then is simply thrown out there on the street to learn from experience.

I have seen instances where cops completely ignored the witness testimony and simply wrote up their report in a way that was most "expedient" for them to be able to move on to the next thing. That can be a challenge in a court setting when the police officer's report says one thing and a real VAR expert says another. There is a basic belief that the police officer made the right decision. Sometimes you are able to catch them early enough in the investigation that you can work with them very closely, agree once all the facts and evidence have been reviewed, and then let them write their report, which will mirror yours. However, that is unfortunately the exception, not the rule. Also, this is a learned skill just like anything else. Would you rather have someone that does 10 accident reconstructions per year, or someone that works on 10 per month?

Timothy D. Christ, M.B.A.

Chapter 15:

CYBER AND FIDELITY CASES

In the last ten years or so, there has been an explosion of cyber-crime and the media coverage surrounding it. It seems every month you hear that another big company got hacked into and released a lot of Personally Identifiable Information (PII) or other protected-by-law information such as Personal Health Information (PHI). Cyber insurance has been introduced by all the major insurance companies because they all love new lines of business.

At first, most of these cyber claims were being filed under Coverage B of the Commercial General Liability policy, also known as advertising injury or media liability. The standard ISO form was re-written to specifically exclude that a few years ago and has forced companies to buy stand-alone cyber policies. There are still some forms out there with "some" cyber coverage in a 1st party property, 3rd party boiler & machinery policy, fidelity bond policies, and others. An article came out within the last couple of years that a tower of

$1 billion cyber insurance policy was built. At the time of this writing, there still has not been the "wide adoption" by the SMB marketplace of a cyber product as of yet, but publicly traded companies are now required to disclose specific cyber concerns and their risk management strategies on their Annual 10-K's.

Cyber claims are a very interesting and technical area because only the information technology (IT) people really understand how computers and systems work. For example, we had a criminal gang that had made a copy of a person's debit card. They were able to use that copied debit card and pull money out of an ATM. They "tested" it one weekend, and then the next weekend, they pulled $2.4 million out of that account. The account only had about $200 in it. The reason for this was that this Latin American bank "reconciled" all transactions on Monday morning. The copied credit card was able to "fool" the loader file, that was used by the bank to check withdrawal ability, thus allowing this criminal gang to make off with a large amount of cash. Most banks have a "fidelity bond" policy which insures the bank in the event any of their employees steal money. It is intended to be first-party coverage to reimburse the bank for employee theft. The fidelity bond policy generally is written in such a way that is only "includes losses" that occur within the physical

Timothy D. Christ, M.B.A.

property or that the "nefarious acts occur within the physical property" of the bank. So, if a hacker penetrates the bank system from the outside and is able to steal money, there is no coverage for that under a Fidelity Bond policy.

Imagine a typical house. There are two doors, a garage door, and say 10 windows on the first floor. Those are your potential entry points for burglars. Now imagine the same house with a family of four. Each person has a cell phone, a car with a lot of electronics in it, likely a computer and/or IPAD, and a work computer that you know they check their personal email and view other websites, shop online, etc. Your house likely has connectivity to the outside world through a WIFI connection, your HVAC might be connected to your local utility, you might have a "SMART home system" that controls everything, etc. All of a sudden, the potential entry points for digital hackers is easily 20 different points of entry or more. The kicker is that no one in that family of four is an IT expert. They don't know how to set up everything in their house to protect themselves as best as possible. The exact same thing goes on in the business world. You've got legacy systems that are 40+ years old, you have 2,000 employees who all have a computer, you have on average 50 different computer programs that are all supposed to talk to one another, you have 5 locations that are all wired a little differently, and a hacker simply has to ask, "What is the best way for me to get into this company?" If they want in, they will get in. We've been involved in cases where an email was sent containing a virus that uploaded keylogging software. The hackers simply waited and "mapped" the infrastructure of the company for months; getting passwords, usernames, etc. Only when they had completely reverse-engineered the company infrastructure did they strike. They were very successful.

Cyber is a brand-new world for a lot of folks that are very limited in their computer literacy. It's going to get a whole lot worse before it gets better. However, the shear brilliance of the way some of the hacks are initiated makes you have to respect their creativity. In the insurance world, insurers are trying to limit coverages by covering "investigation" but not "remediation" or providing coverage caps for each of those respective areas. Timing is important. What if you bought a cyber policy on Jan 1st, but then find out that they actually "hacked" your system in August and were simply waiting to strike? Many companies get hacked through connections with suppliers, and so you have to evaluate your supplier contractual agreements

Timothy D. Christ, M.B.A.

to see if you are including subrogation language in there or are inadvertently giving waivers of subrogation in the event they hack into your system. If you have a 3rd party managing a lot of your IT security and you get hacked, do they have to cover the cleanup costs? The basic questions for coverage still apply. These include such details as the coverage period? Is it a covered loss? What is the trigger for coverage? What is the extent of damage? What are the costs to repair/clean the system? Are there any 3rd party contributory liability factors?

Chapter 16:

PROJECT MANAGEMENT ON LARGE LOSSES

Just because you are very skilled technically has absolutely no bearing on your ability, or inability, to successfully manage large loss projects. In large losses, there are typically multiple technical aspects of the claim, as well as a much more complex investigation process. When losses are large enough there is direct negotiation that must take place with the relevant governmental agencies that may control the site. Communication with the client, instead of simply being with one adjuster, is now a room full of 10-12 parties because of the complexity and nature of the claim. There may be a room full of potentially adverse parties or simply a room full of the players on "the slip" that all share in the property coverage for a single insured, but all are extremely interested in a very definite determination of what the ultimate claim value should really be.

Each party (in an adverse situation) may decide to bring their own expert, and so whoever the coordinating expert is has to successfully manage this group process and maintain control, while at the same time provide the required investigation time, process and accessibility, and, ideally, do so in a manner that brings a complex matter to an expedient resolution, at least from the technical perspective. The goal of any forensic engineer in a large loss scenario is to provide an accurate causation opinion, a narrow cost range for the extent of damage, mitigation options and related costs, and other information as needed by the clients. Also included is the management of the other expert teams so that they can report back (ideally the same information that you determine) with their clients so that there are no differences of opinion on the cause of the incident or the range of values of what is owed. If that can all be established within the first month or two of a large loss, that is ideal. Let the adjusters, carriers, and lawyers debate over contractual agreements, policy coverages, and other case law issues for the next several months or years.

However, if the engineer is not able to provide a quality opinion quickly and manage this process well, then his value as a Large Loss Project Manager drops precipitously. This is a learned skill, so it takes being part of the Large Loss team on several occasions, and gradually being handed more and more direct responsibility before allowing someone to completely bear the full Project Management responsibilities. A rough approximation would be that a person should be directly involved in no less than 20 large losses prior to having any significant responsibilities in one himself. Ideally, he would have been involved in 50 or more, have demonstrated extreme competence under close supervision, and is then turned loose to do Project Management on his own.

Reporting is a completely different animal in large loss scenarios. Daily worksheets as well as weekly summaries should be used. Scopes of work in various phases as well as projected budgets with measurable milestones are crucial to keeping everyone on the same page. Dropbox, ShareFile, and/or Sharepoint pages are key to allowing multiple parties to access all the relevant documentation. Weekly and/or monthly conference calls are typical. Sending out draft inspection protocols before the investigation is performed in order to give each party a complete understanding of what will happen at the date in the future, allowing time for comments, and then providing finalized versions to all parties in advance takes a lot of planning and preparation. Sign-in sheets in order to track attendance, badges to identify each authorized member, and the list goes on and on. Lastly, if there is subrogation potential that is seen early on, and an attorney is involved, attorney-client and work-product issues must be considered.

Chapter 17:

THE LONDON MARKET

At the time of this writing, there are 99 syndicates of the Lloyd's of London who collectively write $35.5 billion pounds of gross premiums. This is the original home of insurance, and it has a very unique style and feel when you go there to conduct business. It is steeped in tradition and it is very important to understand the moving parts. London got its start with a number of blokes sitting around and betting on which ships would actually make it into port. Now it has evolved into a Lego set of building blocks with 62 different color-coded pieces that are all different shapes and sizes and ultimately build a number of different towers.

Timothy D. Christ, M.B.A.

Historically, London is the place that you go to write excess and surplus (E&S) risks. For example, a US low-budget hotel in a bad area of town that doesn't have a fire suppression system because it was built before the building code required it. The vast majority of US insurers wouldn't want to take on that $20 million dollar risk, because they see it as high-risk. For that, the agent representing the owner has to go to the E&S market. London will issue a policy, but you'll see 12-15 various companies share in the $20 million dollar policy.

Lloyd's is an intermediary that connects the global insurance market to the 62 syndicate members mentioned above. Each syndicate decides what types of risks they want to insure.

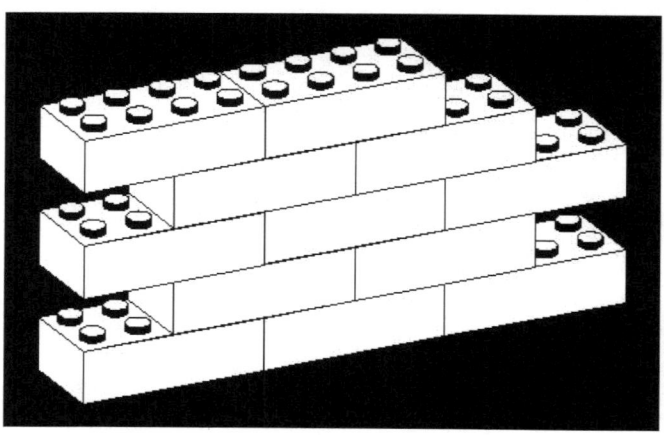

Becoming an Expert: The Business of Forensic Engineering

London can also be viewed as the ultimate chess match. Let's take a company like Apple, for example, that has billions of dollars in assets all over the world. Apple will self-insure the first, say $25 million of any losses that arise each year. This is also known as their Self-Insured Retention (SIR) or in typical residential insurance policy-speak, it is their deductible. If Apple wanted to set up a Captive Insurance Company (which is simply a subsidiary of their company that provides insurance back to the parent company), typically to provide significant tax and expense savings, then whatever amount of risk they are willing to take on, they will self-insure.

There are a couple ways this plays out. Apple's broker will go to the market and say, I want $2 billion in coverage. AIG, since they like to "lead" (which means be the first or primary coverage holder), will say, I'll take the risk from your SIR of $25 million up to $75 million. That is typically known as the "primary insurance layer." Additional companies will then also take slivers of the risk from $76 million up through $2 billion. That is called "excess" coverage.

Depending upon the claims history of the insured, you may find a few companies competing in this arena or a lot. Sometimes a full LEGO tower of coverage could contain 15-25 different companies. The piece of paper that contains all the carrier information and their respective % of coverage is called "the slip."

In the above example, AIG will then buy re-insurance to help further diffuse the risk of several Apple losses for that $25-75 million swath that they have just written. The challenge for primary insurers is the balancing act of retaining risk (and the premium dollars) and purchasing adequate reinsurance. For every dollar of reinsurance that you buy that you never use, you have lost both direct profit from that $1 as well as the value of the "float" that it would have given you.

If you think the brokering process is complicated, wait until there is a claim for say $751 million. Then all of a sudden you've got 16 clients instead of just one like you would for a $10 million claim. The positive side is that once you've worked on a number of really large losses involving multiple players in the market, you can better "sell" them on new claims because they are already familiar with your work on previous losses.

What is most important to know about London is who controls the claims and who are the influencers. The people that "control" the claims process, and by default the investigation, is generally the lead insurer. If a claim grows to a particularly large number, then you can have some interesting claims conversations about settlement and the appropriate value of settlement, because the higher you go, the more parties you involve. As insurers are in the business of paying claims, as long as there is good justification for it, it's fine.

If you spend any time at all in London or in larger claims, the concept of re-insurance will soon come up. There are two primary types of reinsurance, facultative and treaty. Facultative is intended to cover a specific risk or group of risks within the primary insurer. Treaty generally means insurance purchased to cover all risks within a specific insurance class.

Since London writes policies all over the world, there can be regional differences as well. For example, a US insurance carrier may write a $50 million policy for a US-based property. However, if that property is located in Mexico, many times the primary insurance carrier in Mexico (also known as the fronting company) might only actually retain 1% of that risk, or a mere $500,000. 99% of that risk is then re-insured, i.e. sold into London. Munich Re might take the first 25-30% of that risk and then it gets divided up by the syndicates from there. In the Mexico example, Munich RE would then control the claim and investigation process, with the assistance of the local fronting company. Most countries require that insurance be written through a nationally-based company, so that is why you'll see a number of very small "locally insured risks" (or as a percentage of the total risk) insured by a local insurance company. As markets mature, and the ability to properly forecast and predict likely losses increase, you'll typically see a rise in local retention rates. This is why you have seen London put satellite offices into developing economies, because the greatest opportunity for London to grow its top-line revenue is to sell more policies in areas where sufficient levels of insurance is difficult to acquire.

Chapter 18:

THE BASICS OF LITIGATION

The first question is, do you need an expert? In some litigated cases, expert witnesses are not needed. Expert witnesses are needed when there are one of a few major issues:

1. There are disputed questions of fact, or in other words, potential differing opinions on the proximate cause of the incident in question. Did Driver A cause the vehicle collision or did Driver B?
2. There are disputed opinions relating to the magnitude of the incident in question. Is it a $1,000 claim or a $1 million claim?
3. You have poor fact witnesses and you feel like an independent, third-party, objective expert would add credibility to explaining the circumstances of the situation.
4. Other…

Timothy D. Christ, M.B.A.

In some litigated cases, the lawyers can put the parties or various involved persons on the witness stand to establish sequence of events, fact patterns, etc., and allow the jury to interpret for themselves. However, for potentially large claim amounts, or for more complex fact issues, bringing in the appropriate expert witnesses can be highly valuable.

The absolute first step in hiring an expert is a conflict check. Many lawyers will say, "I know you are not currently involved in this case, so we are fine." That is incorrect. The conflict check needs to uncover whether or not we are currently involved in that case (as a consulting expert, in which case, we haven't been disclosed to the other side), as well as have we ever worked for or against any of the parties in the past and what was the nature of the relationship? If a lawyer is suing AIG, and AIG is a $5 million/year client of mine, I'm going to ask their permission prior to accepting the project. However, I also want the lawyer retaining my services to understand my relationships with any of the parties. Everything will come out in trial, so it is much more advantageous to be up-front and honest about any concerns either side has. This is why it is extremely important to ask any expert witness firm what background checks, degree verification checks, and other information do they obtain about their experts. A couple quick war stories to highlight this:

I had a brand-new expert I had just contracted with for a case in South Texas. He is probably the 4th most qualified expert in his field, but he lied on his CV when he wrote that he graduated from college. He took 2.5 years of classes but never graduated. Thankfully, my internal HR department caught it before we had signed him up for the client. We amended his CV and sent the information over in its true format. The client agreed to the expert and we proceeded. That case ultimately settled, but had we gone to trial, opposing council would have researched that and it would have made our expert look like a complete liar had we not caught it in time.

A second war story was a 23-year employee that I had and was put forth as a testifying expert on a file that he worked. Opposing council did their job, and revealed to us that our expert had multiple, recent DWI's. He was never anything but professional in our presence. However, our attorney and our client were concerned about the recent nature of two of them. I agreed 100%. We did a full background check, degree verification, credit check, and other, but they were done at the time of hire, not every year. That brings up an interesting point. Should a third-party service provider perform a complete review on each employee annually or every 3-5 years?

If the expert witness firm is any good, the first thing they will ask for is a copy of the latest amended petition and the certificate of service. This accomplishes three things. First, is that some lawyers shop experts. I have zero interest in spending my time responding to a lawyer that most likely will not engage my firm. If I ask for something as simple as these court documents, and they refuse, the odds of them engaging my firm decreased by 90+%. If they were serious, they would understand and appreciate the request. Second, what it does is provide me with the background details of the case: who, what, when, where, why, and how. It also provides me with the various legal theories for which the parties are being sued. In early petitions, most lawyers will include everything, expecting to reduce the actual claims at some point in the litigation process. For an expert, the types of allegations are invaluable. You can quickly determine if there is something that you can assist with that most likely would allow you to be non-suited, provide the judge with enough reason to rule in your favor on a Motion for Summary Judgment, or other legal wrangling that could potentially get your client out of the proceedings. Third, if for any reason the original attorney does not want to contract with me, the certificate of service provides the contact details of all the other lawyers and parties involved in the matter, and I can call them directly, introduce myself, explain that I am aware of this pending litigation they are involved in, and offer my assistance.

From the expert perspective, you have to understand the evolution of case law and how it impacts expert testimony. You should be able to explain in great detail the Frye case from 1922. Frye ushered in the "general acceptance standard." You should be able to explain in detail the Federal Rules of Evidence 701, 702, and 703. If you are in Federal Court you will have to submit a Rule 26A disclosure. You should be able to explain the Daubert and Kumho Tire cases and how they apply to FEDERAL court testimony. Daubert held that Frye was inconsistent with Rule 702, and held that the court is the "gatekeeper" and encouraged a more liberal approach to expert testimony. Kumho held that the gatekeeper "reliability standard" be used for any knowledge that is expert witness testimony. You should be able to explain the local STATE court ruling, such as Robinson in Texas, which is the follow-up to the Daubert case. Robinson brought in the idea that the opinion should be based on a reasonable foundation. You should be able to explain the continuation of Texas

Supreme Court state case law with cases such as Gammill. You should be able to discuss the Texas Practice and Remedies Code 74 and other sections as necessary.

Each potential expert witness should be evaluated against common criteria:

1. Does the expert have the right expertise for our case?
2. To what extent does the expert have experience related to this particular type of situation?
3. Has the expert ever been disqualified?
4. How many times has the expert offered testimony (and what is the win/loss ratio)?
5. How does the expert come across? Scholarly? In a professorial manner? In an arrogant manner?
6. For the grey areas of my case, which way are they willing to lean and how does that impact the "scientific nature" or validity of their findings?

Most cases go to mediation once or twice prior to actually getting a trial setting. The most successful mediations that I have ever seen involve bringing the expert to the mediation. It was quite common for me to sit with the opposing plaintiff expert, agree as to causes, extent of damage, and repair options, provide a range (high-low) back to our respective counsels, and then let them negotiate from there. The less successful ones are typically those where counsel is not prepared or not willing to "show their hand" Or where the defense shows up with no settlement authority, thus wasting everyone's time. This means they don't want to give the other side all the information they can bring up in trial because they feel like they can slam them with this information at trial. In rare cases is the other side surprised by information provided at trial. Good opposing counsel will investigate thoroughly to understand the strengths and weaknesses of a case. The added benefit of having the experts at the mediation is the ability to have their opinions updated immediately by any new information provided, or at least to have them provide a range to their attorney of what is substantiated vs. what is not. It can be extremely effective to prepare animations/trial presentations to show the other side in order to help the attorney on the other side convince their clients of the relative weaknesses they have in certain areas.

Depositions are typically the next step in litigation proceedings. Occasionally, there will be a few key depositions performed prior to a mediation. For an expert giving testimony, there is both an art and a science to giving a deposition. You need to understand what your client's goals are related to your deposition. You need to have discussed the defensible areas and the gray areas of your opinions with counsel representing your party. You should have practiced potential answers to questions the other counsel is likely to raise. A great deposition can be a death sentence to the opposing counsel. However, if it is not done correctly, it merely prolongs the process and costs everyone more money. The attorney asking all the questions is attempting to box in the expert to a narrow interpretation, or try to get them to admit to other potential causes. An expert that is highly skilled and well-practiced can answer in such a manner that his theory of the cause is the only one that jury believes, thus leaving the opposing expert with little room to maneuver. This is why it is an art, and not a science. There are 5 or more ways to answer a question or a series of questions, but only one or two typically put your client in the positive leverage position following a deposition.

Of course, only 1-2% of all cases go to trial. And of those, about 60% or better settle on the courthouse steps. So, the correct focus of the defense counsel is to both prepare for trial, but also give the other side every reason in the world to not do so. The trial is so much different than the previous steps, especially if you are in federal court. In state court cases, you get a jury of 12 with typically a median of a high school education. They don't necessarily want to be there but they have showed up. In either situation, your job as attorney is to give them a show that they can enjoy, tell them a story they believe, and, at the end, have enough information to cast an informed vote. This is where you want to bring out the CSI examples of videos/animations, charts, graphs, and photos. You want to practice with your expert so that they look at the jury, entertain them, engage them, teach them, and ultimately become credible and gain agreement by the jury.

Timothy D. Christ, M.B.A.

Chapter 19:

BUILDING A GREAT ENGINEERING TEAM

Looking back on my development, I recognize that "trial by fire" is a good, but not great training program. The nice thing about Catastrophe (CAT) situations is that there are so many files that everyone is buried. The first 50 or so files that I did produced poor-to-mediocre quality reports. Thankfully, I was able to successfully manage to a mutually agreeable solution in mediation, and so the poor quality nature of the reports did not negatively impact my client. I had the rough outline of the information I needed, and with some input from the other side, was able to successfully fill in the blanks in order to arrive at supportable conclusions.

However, if I have 100 or 1,000 hail claims to investigate, it's perfectly okay to have a junior structural engineer that doesn't know much go cut his teeth on 50-100 of those. Once he gets to 50, he'll be a whole lot better than he was on his first 5. Now, I completely agree that I should provide some training on the front end of that, as well as institute quality control procedures to make his first 50 files as technically correct as possible. In a CAT situation he'll do 50 inspections in two weeks, whereas normally it might take six months or more to acquire the same amount of on-the-job training.

The ideal training situation would be a CAT where I could take a junior engineer on his first 20 or so inspections, have him simply follow me around, take notes, keep his mouth shut, and then ask questions when we leave the site. After 20, I would start assigning him particular tasks for the next 30 or so. I would gradually turn over all the tasks to him while having him be under my direct supervision. Once he demonstrated competence in all areas of the inspection and report development process, I would turn him loose to conduct joint inspections with other engineers. That way he'd learn from multiple styles and viewpoints. After another 30 or so of those, I'd turn him loose to conduct some solo inspections, with the direction that if any unanticipated or strange situation occurs, to call immediately. Once an engineer gets a couple hundred inspections under their belt, they'll develop a pretty good level of confidence and expertise. Then the idea is to cross-train them on other types of claim scenarios.

Timothy D. Christ, M.B.A.

Send a Structural Engineer on some environmental claims, some mechanical claims, and some electrical claims. They will not be primary on the site, but the idea is for them to learn the "complete forensic engineering thought process" because it is the same process regardless of the type of claim. Also, it will make them more well-rounded in their experience and they'll be more prepared to do Project Management, where they manage a team of engineers on a single loss as opposed to simply conducting a number of investigations by themselves.

They need to spend some time in all aspects of the business process. They need to spend time with the sales/marketing people on the front end so they can hear directly from clients and prospects how they like for their service providers to work and report to them. They need to train other engineers, because until you teach it, you have not mastered it. They need to do quality control and report review of other engineers. This helps them identify things they like that they will incorporate into their work, and they'll also identify common deficiencies which will enhance the quality of everyone's reports. They need to spend some time dealing with the lawyers on litigated matters, so they understand the language difference between claims and litigation. They also need to understand the lawyer's priorities vs. the claim adjuster's priorities, as they are not the same.

This type of holistic training is a minimum 3-year process, and to truly achieve mastery of it takes at least 5 years. A person can be a decent engineer for 20 years and never develop to world-class status. They have to have the internal desire to continually refine and develop their craft. There is a popular quote that says, one guy got 20 years' worth of experience, and another guy got one year's worth of experience 20 times. That is very true in the forensic engineering business as well. Some people have been doing it the same way for 20 years, and if that is the case, then they have utterly failed in continuing to sharpen their saw.

An excellent way to measure a person's true ability is to assign them claims that are outside their comfort zone. If they can successfully navigate and manage any type of project you throw at them, then they have developed to world-class status. If there is extreme push-back from the consultant and they only want to handle a certain type of claim, then you know that you have a person that will not develop to the level you want unless they change their attitude.

Chapter 20:

THE CHANGING LANDSCAPE OF INSURANCE

There are a number of books out that talk about the future of insurance. We hear all the time about cloud computing, machine learning (ML), artificial intelligence (AI), robotic process automation (RPA), data analytics, and more. I'd point to my friends Rob Galbraith and his book "The End of Insurance As We Know It," or Bryan Falchuk's book, "The Future of Insurance: From Disruption to Evolution."

The point that I want to draw you to is this. In the book, Competing on Data Analytics, published by the Harvard Business Press, they talk about the concept that as the degree of intelligence about your business goes up, your competitive advantage increases. What this means is that for those carriers who are better able to develop systems and processes to access their own data, put it into complex algorithmic calculations, predictive modeling scenarios, and more, will be the more successful and profitable businesses going forward.

Many carriers have legacy mainframe computers, and even for those who are newer/more sophisticated, they generally have multiple data sets lying in separate areas. The primary challenge faced by an insurer is two-fold:

1. How do I integrate all my various data sets together?
2. What data sets do I choose to start with?

As we talked about in the insurance business model chapter, speed is of the essence. Any software program that fits any of the following criteria is cause for serious evaluation:

- Is faster than current processing state
- Provides lower error rate than current processing
- Provides greater granularity in terms of coding the various data points in order to provide better, detailed reports

From an insurer perspective, as they are evaluating the strategy on how to upgrade their current systems and processes, most often the strategic plan emerges with two primary goals:

1. Ensuring that the basic platform is robust enough to handle the future enhanced state. To use my home-building analogy, it doesn't matter how pretty the roof is if the foundation sucks. In any infrastructure discussion, there are basic foundational and fundamental elements that must come first.
2. Which components offer the greatest return-on-investment?

This gets complicated because of the various factors in play. If you swap out one part of your system, what other departments or areas will be affected by that change? You may have a large ROI, but if the interdependency of other departments causes the timeline to be significantly delayed, then your ROI is measurably reduced.

Logically is another way of developing the plan. What occurs first? Let's fix the first thing in the chain, then the 2nd link, and then continue until we've fixed all links in the chain and then start over again. To continue with our analogy of the insurance company's claims process acting like a bullet train, if you can speed up First Notice of Loss (FNOL), claim assignment, vendor notification, etc., then you speed up everything that happens after that. In a separate example, there is software that provides significant savings for litigated files. However, if your "bigger decision" is not to do both, but to do one first, which makes more sense?

We can speed up the claims process, which reduces litigation spend. Or we can reduce litigation spend, but not fundamentally change anything about our claims process?

If we invest in the litigation spend first, because it's convenient, then we save x% per year. If however, we speed up the claims process which reduces the total number of litigated files per year, then our litigation software solution just became less valuable. Speed is also a key variable here. If we can implement the litigation software in 90 days and see returns immediately, and we know that automating our claims system will be a 5-7 year plan, then we might as well reap the savings of the litigation savings in the meantime.

My argument is not that you shouldn't do both, but you should evaluate carefully the order in which you do things, because there will be higher priority items and lower priority items, as no company can do them all at the same time.

Chapter 21:

CONCLUSION

I hope that this book helps to shortcut the learning curve of anyone else that is in this business. This is truly a wonderful business in which to be in. There are some really interesting people with whom you get to work, some incredible places to visit, and endless opportunities to continue to learn new things, and tremendous development opportunities to grow professionally, personally, financially, etc.! I have loved every minute of it. The latest articles indicate that the average millennial might have 15-20 different employers during their working careers! Wow! Just 20 years ago it was commonplace for a person to have started with a company, put in their 30-40 years, and retire. How does a millennial successfully navigate 15-20 companies, bosses, co-workers, vendors, responsibilities, etc.?

You get comfortable with being uncomfortable. As Yoda might say, "You become one with change." I learned this a long time ago and continue to learn the

Becoming an Expert: The Business of Forensic Engineering

lesson daily. I was playing professional golf, just out of college, and completely at peace with what I was doing. A guy comes along, starts playing golf with me, finds out about my business and marketing degree, and tries to recruit me into his forensic engineering company. "No thanks, I'm a professional golfer." He keeps after me, I decide that I should probably get a real job, and I go to work for him. I'm a golfer, not an engineer. I don't know anything about engineering. So, I learned. I asked a ton of questions of some really smart people and I got comfortable being the dumbest guy in the room, because I literally was.

Our three biggest clients re-wrote their insurance policies excluding Foundation Coverage from the policies, and, overnight, we lost 95% of our business. We laid off 23 people. They promoted me to Marketing Manager at the exact same time and said, "your job is to rebuild our business." I'd never built any businesses before. 1.5 years ago, I was a professional golfer, and now I've been an Engineering Technician for a short while. So, I learned. I talked to every single person that would talk to me, asked a lot of questions, and along the way, was able to bring in enough new litigation work to sustain our small office.

Timothy D. Christ, M.B.A.

I started to get the hang of the forensic engineering business, and so I looked across the border into Mexico and said, "surely, they have all the same issues we have in the US, right? Shouldn't we be doing some work there?" I went into Reynosa which is right across the border from McAllen, and talked to some insurance people. They said, "you have to go to Monterrey." So, I went to Monterrey. They said. "you have to go to Mexico City." So, I went to Mexico City. I started bringing in quite a bit of new work. My dream became to open a Mexico City office, hire local staff, and make it successful. A kid that grew up on a farm, never spoke any language but English, knows nothing about international business, but is going to plant an operation in another country. Why not? My parents always told me I could do anything I set my mind to.

I transferred to the San Antonio office, which was losing money at the time, and was asked to help them turnaround their operation. I'd been successful doing it in McAllen once, so at least this time, I had part of an idea of what to do. I went to work, not knowing exactly what I was doing, but I had confidence that I could figure it out. 8 months after I was there, we broke even, and in another year, we cleared a $250,000 profit.

Becoming an Expert: The Business of Forensic Engineering

I took an opportunity to help another firm go from a local client base to a regional client base. I had never done that for an accounting firm before, but I said, "sure, I can figure that out." I went to work. I built them a million-dollar pipeline in 8 months. I got a call from another forensic engineering firm saying we want you to come run our Forensic Engineering Division and we want to grow in Latin America. It was nirvana for me. I hired a couple of my old employees and we were off to the races. We built it up, hired local staff, and planted an operation there. 13 years out of college and here I was, CEO of an operation in Mexico that I dreamed about and founded.

They asked me to open their Western Canadian operation. What do I know about building business in Canada? Nothing, but I can learn. They do have gorgeous golf courses up there, so that was a big plus. They asked me to build an Energy Practice. What do I know about Energy? Next to nothing, but I can learn. Now I have been a featured speaker at four Insurance Risk Management Institute (IRMI) Energy Risk Conferences held annually in Texas. They asked me to build Cyber Practice. What do I know about Cyber? Even less, but I can learn. It was really neat that our Cyber Practice evolved into both a Cyber and Fidelity Claims Practice. Sometimes when you are working really hard you just get lucky, and that is basically what happened. We were referred into a Fidelity Claims Organization, they fell in love with our expertise and services, and we became a serious player in the technical investigation of Fidelity Claims. The moral of the story? Three quotes come to mind that have defined my life:

#1. Shoot for the moon and if you miss you are still among stars.

#2: If you're not living life on the edge, you're taking up too much space.

#3. Life begins at the end of your comfort zone.

I don't even know what my comfort zone is anymore. Actually, that is not true. My comfort zone is when I'm pushing boundaries and helping others to achieve more than they ever thought possible. What is most gratifying today is to look back and see all those folks that have realized extraordinary success because we pushed our limits:

- A small-town civil engineer becomes a Practice Leader and managed thousands of high volume/low severity property and storm damage claims. He quadruples his annual income.

Becoming an Expert: The Business of Forensic Engineering

- A small-town police officer becomes the Practice Leader for all Motorcycle Claims. He doubles his annual income.

- A small-town fire marshal becomes CEO of a Mexican company and the premier fire investigator in all Latin America. He quadruples his annual income.

- A small-town engineer becomes an internationally-renowned Cyber and Fidelity Claims Expert. He doubles his annual income.

- An internationally-born engineer gets to do what he loved, travel throughout Latin America and work on massive claims, God rest his soul.

- A Petroleum Engineer becomes an internationally-recognized Energy Expert.

- A Mexican Electrical Engineer has now traveled extensively throughout Latin America working on several very significant, large losses.

I'm reminded of one last quote: "Two roads diverged in a yellow wood...I took the one less traveled by, and that has made all the difference." I pray that you are able to get comfortable being uncomfortable, and go

Timothy D. Christ, M.B.A.

accomplish something that you never even dreamed about doing. If you like, I'm happy to help. After my faith and my family, it's my favorite thing to do.

I'll leave you with the letter I wrote to my Mexico employees and other Latin America colleagues upon my retirement. The first letter is obviously in Spanish, because that is my second language and is a language that I have come to love as much as English. The English version is behind it.

Becoming an Expert: The Business of Forensic Engineering

Estimados Colegas y Amigos,

En primer lugar, gracias por su esfuerzo diario. Ustedes siempre han sido y siempre serán la parte más importante de esta empresa. Cuando tuve el sueño de crear esta empresa en México y América Latina, quería construir algo grande que durara más que el momento de mi estancia aquí. Traje en el mejor equipo de diseño del mundo para ayudar a diseñar y construir la mejor y más fuerte compañía posible. Yo contrate a los mejores talentos en el mundo para trabajar, y en última instancia, conducir esta empresa. Siento cada uno de ustedes como mis propios miembros de la familia, y tengo las más altas esperanzas de que continuará su desarrollo y superación incluso sueños muy grandes.

Yo los formé para que siempre pongan su integridad en primer lugar, al cliente en un segundo lugar muy cercano, y los beneficios en un distante tercer lugar. Siempre han demostrado los más altos niveles de integridad, e incluso aunque usted no se da cuenta, esto es visto por nuestros clientes. Aun cuando en ocasiones hemos fallado, hemos pedido disculpas y continuamos trabajando para mejorar. Los clientes van a seguir y seguir haciendo negocios con ustedes. Ellos ven cuando usted está poniendo sus intereses sobre nuestros beneficios, y no hay más "valioso" proveedor de servicios en el mundo que eso. Siempre he creído, y lo han vivido, que los beneficios llegarán cuando haces todo lo mejor de su capacidad. La alegría más grande que he tenido es enviar esos cheques para ustedes, y escucharlos decir: "estos son los bonos más grandes que hemos recibido."

Mi ferviente esperanza es que usted pueda seguir creciendo, para desarrollar y dar más oportunidades a otras personas trabajar en esta empresa. Cuídense el uno al otro; estos son los miembros de su familia ahora, no sólo "amigos del trabajo." Ustedes han sudado juntos, sangrado juntos, estado enfermo juntos, y juntos sobresalido. Ustedes logran más de lo que cualquier es capaz de lograr solo. Para mí fue un honor y un privilegio trabajar con ustedes todos los días. He aprendido mucho más de ustedes de lo que nunca he logrado solo de mí. La preocupación de todos los Directores Generales es que, en algún momento, su presencia puede frenar la creatividad y/o la oportunidad de sus empleados, por lo que la elección más difícil para él es cuándo le toca salir.

Para mí, todos ustedes saben la razón. Las únicas responsabilidades que son mayores que esta empresa son mi fe y mi familia. Mi esposa necesita a su marido, y mi pequeño niño necesita a su padre. Estando ausente más del 85% del tiempo, no nos hace un esposo o padre responsable. Así que he tomado la decisión, al mismo tiempo, más dura, y más fácil que he tenido que hacer. Les deseo lo mejor y sé que todo lo que tenía disponible para dar, lo he dado a ustedes. Tengo grandes esperanzas en ustedes. Gracias por los regalos que me han dado, sus corazones, sus mentes, su tiempo, su creatividad, y lo más importante, su amistad. Saben que es lo que yo agradezco más.

Pd. Como su jefe, es lógico que les deje con algunas instrucciones finales:

1. Continuar soñando con lo que puede lograrse, y trabajar diligentemente para lograrlo.

2. Mantener, o, preferiblemente, mejorar la disciplina fiscal con la que hemos operado.

3. No crecer por crecer, más bien, encontrar gente buena y darles la oportunidad de sobresalir.

4. Tratar a los demás con el mismo cuidado y la compasión con la que os he tratado

5. Encontrar nuevos clientes que puedan servir y superar sus expectativas

6. Sea generoso con su tiempo, talentos, tesoros y posesiones

7. Desarrollar nuestros empleados y compañeros de trabajo con la satisfacción de que el día que le toque irse, los deje preparados para continuar con la misión

8. Celebrar con sus familias los frutos de su trabajo

Becoming an Expert: The Business of Forensic Engineering

Dear Colleagues and Friends,

First of all, thank you for all that you do every day. You have always been and will always be the most important part of this company. When I had the dream for this Mexico company, I wanted to build something that would outlast my time here. I brought in the world's best design team to help me design and build the best, strongest possible company. I recruited and hired the best talent in the world to work in, and ultimately lead, this company. I love each of you as my own family members, and have the highest hopes that you will continue your development and exceed even your wildest dreams.

I trained you so that you always put your integrity first, the customer a very close second, and profits a distant third. You have always shown the highest levels of integrity, and even if you don't realize it, it is seen by our clients. Even when we have occasionally failed, we apologized and continued to work to get better. The clients will follow and continue to do business with you. They see when you are putting their interests over your profits, and there is no more "valuable" service provider in the world than that. I have always believed, and you have lived it, that profits will come when you do everything else to the best of your ability. The greatest joy I have ever had was writing those checks to you, and having you say, "these are the biggest bonuses we have ever received."

My fervent hope is for you to continue to grow, develop, and provide opportunity for more people to work in this company. Take care of each other; these are your family members now, not just "work friends." You have sweated together, bled together, been sick together, and excelled together. You together are greater than what any are able to achieve apart. It was my distinct honor and privilege to work among you every day. I learned far more from you than you ever did from me. Every CEO's concern is that at some point, his/her presence may stifle the creativity and opportunity of his people, and so the most difficult choice for him is not if, but when to leave.

For me, you all know the reason. The only responsibilities that are greater than this company are my faith and my family. My wife needs her husband, and my little toddler needs his dad. Being gone 85%+ of the time is not being a responsible husband or father. So, I made the decision that was, at the same time, the hardest, and easiest decision that I have ever had to make. I wish you the best and know that everything I had available to give, I gave to you. I have high hopes for you. Thank you for the gifts you have given me, your hearts, your minds, your time, your creativity, and most importantly, your friendship. Know that is what I will cherish the most.

P.S. As your boss, it's only fitting that I leave you with some final instructions:

1. Continue to dream about what can be achieved, and work diligently toward achieving it.

2. Maintain, or preferably enhance the fiscal discipline with which we have operated under.

3. Do not grow for growth's sake, rather, find good people and give them the opportunity to excel.

4. Treat each other with the same care and compassion with which I have treated you.

5. Find new clients who you can serve and exceed their expectations.

6. Be generous of your time, talents, treasures, and possessions.

7. Develop our people with the expectation that one day you will leave too, and have them prepared to carry on the mission.

8. Celebrate with your families the fruits of your labor.

Thank you very much for reading this book. I hope that you learned something. The question now for you is, what will be your mountain to climb? What can you do that will make a difference in several other people's lives, and ultimately, make a significant difference in yours? You can connect with me at www.linkedin.com/in/timothydavidchrist or on Facebook. I look forward to hearing your story.

ABOUT THE AUTHOR

Tim Christ is the Vice President at Claimatic, a SaaS InsurTech that is automating the claims process using AI and ML to drive better claims experiences, faster claims resolutions, a higher value of accuracy in resolution, and reduce both indemnity costs as well as LAE.

He is the retired Director General (Chief Executive Officer in English) of LWG Consulting Mexico, S.A. de C.V. He worked at Rimkus Consulting Group from 2001-2009 and at LWG Consulting (now Envista Forensics) from 2010-2015. He is the first person to open an international forensic engineering office in Latin America and has been recognized as a Power 50, one of the 50 most influential individuals in Latin America.

He is a past speaker in the Lloyd's Library in London, Property Loss Research Bureau (PLRB) Annual Conference, IRMI Energy Risk Conference, and several other national and regional association events. He resides in San Antonio, TX with his wife Betty and their now 7-year old son, Kaleb, who, is the Most Valuable Player for both his Flag Football and Basketball teams, plays Select Baseball, and is rapidly developing into a good junior golfer.

Made in the USA
Columbia, SC
15 October 2021

46917035R00090